"Welcome to the extraordinary community of Sólheimar Ecovillage, where the mundane is transformed into the remarkable, and each resident has the opportunity to find their own right place within a rich variety of community, creativity, and connection. Situated in the heart of Iceland, individuals with diverse neurological backgrounds are offered a safe place where they are not merely embraced but are celebrated for their unique talents.

In this book, Chuck unveils the secrets to cultivating a dynamic, inclusive community where everyone has the opportunity to creatively, intellectually, and emotionally flourish. From the shared pleasures of communal dining to the profound impact of meaningful labor, Sólheimar embraces the essence of purpose-driven existence.

This volume can serve as a guidebook for officials, architects, or relatives eager to delve into and draw inspiration from the stories of Sólheimar's residents and founder. Their dedication, resourcefulness, and sometimes-quirky ways have provided insights into the power of acceptance, respect, and a sense of belonging on individual and collective levels—illustrating how to transform these ideals into tangible realities.

Please join on this journey of an eye-opening exploration into the potential of communal living. Together, let us imagine a future where every individual is encouraged and empowered to lead a life filled with purpose and significance."

Laura Juvik, *Architect, Board Member of Bofællesskab.dk (Danish Cohousing Association), and mother of two autistic children*

"Maxine Greene, educational philosopher, author, and social activist wrote: 'This is what we shall look for as we move: freedom developed by human beings who have acted to make a space for themselves in the presence of others, human beings become "challengers" ready for alternatives, alternatives that include caring and community . . . We want to discover how to open spaces for persons in their plurality, spaces where they can become different, where they can grow. It is important to hold in mind . . . that the person – that center of choice – develops in [their] fullness to a degree [they are] a member of a live community.'

Charles Durrett's most recent book, *Neuro-Inclusive Community Design*, brings Greene's words to life. Through Sólheimar, he describes an example of how the power of intentional community enriches lives, provides opportunities, and creates space for people to simply be who they are."

Laurie Frank, *Cohousing USA Board President*

"As one who is on the path to starting a neuro-inclusive community, I found that *Neuro-Inclusive Community Design* examines this topic very thoroughly. It is both inspirational and practical. The chapters on architecture, economics and the workshops were particularly interesting to me. If you read this, your dreams and ambitions will grow!"

Philip A. DesJardins, *Founding Member of the new forming Grass Valley Neurodivergent Community*

I0866908

"Many of us when we come face-to-face with individuals suffering from neurological challenges, autism or Down syndrome for instance, we look the other way. But Charles Durrett does not do that—in this terrific book. It provides the story of a marvelous community in Iceland that embraces 'the others'. A truly important and fascinating book."

Steve E. Wax, *Reader*

"This is a book that only Charles Durrett could have written. As an architect who specializes in innovative co-housing designs, he is in a unique position to lay before us the special features and particulars of Sólheimar Ecovillage, a neuro-inclusive community in southern Iceland. It has a proven track record of turning those individuals into productive and happy members of the community, reciprocating the love and support they receive from it."

Alfred North, *Reader*

"The book *Neuro-Inclusive Community Design: Lessons from Sólheimar Ecovillage* is a success story about an amazing group of neurodivergent people who are fortunate. I personally am a quadruple amputee. I occasionally need a little help from my friends. Charles Durrett's book paints a picture of such a vibrant, loving community that I wish I could visit. I actually couldn't put this book down, and it's football season!"

Marjie Curry, *Librarian*

"I found this to be both incredibly inspired and compassionate, having ordered several additional copies to share with partners and like-minded advocates. In addition to this being a great case study for interdependent community, the author's reflections on appropriate use of language and their personal story about learning to embrace ADHD resonated with me. It is critical that we find the space to share our own stories of growth and challenges to normalize these conversations and shine light on the beauty of human diversity."

Brian Squillace, *Architect*

"Charles Durrett, disciple, guru, and pied piper of cohousing, has written an excellent book on building community for and with neurodivergent people. Parents of neurodivergent people often search for the non-institutional home that will continue to serve their children after their supporting family is gone. But Durrett's model goes further, showing us how these communities should nest inside all our medium and larger communities as well. The book is thorough and has a helpful chapter on the economics of decisions in these communities. An important tool for your community-building tool chest."

Dan Slone, *Development Legal Consultant*

"Charles Durrett's *Neuro-Inclusive Community Design* is a refreshing and insightful read. What really stands out is how he emphasizes that good design isn't just about the buildings themselves but about how those spaces bring people together.

Reading this book reminded me of the Orangi Town Project in Karachi. There, communities came together to essentially build and run their neighborhoods. Without waiting for the government, residents took matters into their own hands—building sewers, schools, and community spaces. Just like Durrett's cohousing projects, the success of Orangi Town was rooted in the fact that people had a direct stake in shaping their surroundings. It wasn't about flashy architecture or top-down planning, but about creating a sustainable, livable environment based on the needs of the community."

Shamila Zubairi, *AIA, Adjunct Professor*

"In *Neuro-Inclusive Community Design*, Durrett tells the remarkable story of Sólheimar, a cohousing community in Iceland for people with intellectual/developmental disabilities. If you think you won't relate, you're mistaken. Durrett weaves an enthralling story of love and creativity nurtured by a combination of independence and interdependence that allows both residents and staff to thrive. With evocative pictures and an engaging narrative, this is a well-organized book that will inspire similar cohousing communities in the US."

Suzanne Marriott, *Senior Cohousing Co-developer and author*

"Chuck deeply and creatively opens a less-considered view of life to us. This renowned author brings his extensive cohousing development experience to Sólheimar as well as his innate empathy toward his fellow world rumblers there — 'others' he seldom hangs with though he vulnerably includes himself as other."

Betsy Morris, *Cohousing Coach and EcoVillage Ambassador*

"It should be no surprise that Charles Durrett's devotion to cohousing would spread to the neurodiverse population. His investigation and research into the 94-year-old Icelandic community of Sólheimar presents an inspiration and a model to be repeated. Sólheimar is not a lonely warehousing of the disabled, but an opportunity for supportive interdependence with useful purpose for an intentional, select group of people. This optimized environment for mainly the autistic and Down syndrome affected, includes rituals and routines based on program needs and goals including activities such as handcraft workshops with gallery, theater, cooking, maintenance, gardening and forestry. The contribution of work efforts gives purpose and confidence to the individuals at a softer and safe pace and the results show in the smiles and participation levels. I can imagine the relief of family members when their loved one settles into this location with confidence of their lifelong care from a stable staff.

Architectural design supports the intentional community with expansive acreage, multiple buildings all within walking distance, no cars needed. Individuals walk between buildings to visit friends, dine, create pottery, and complete self-selected work assignments. Truly an inspiration to see an alternative to walled-off boxes of humans. Surely, this can be replicated."

Janet Palmer, *Senior Cohousing Resident and Co-Developer*

"As the father of a 35-year-old adult child with autism, what I loved about this book was the reality of community for people with intellectual/developmental disabilities. This blessed book is a lifesaver in providing a sense of possibility . . . reality-based hope. This is also a guiding star for us caregivers. Good mix of story and data – very persuasive. Truly, truly, an inspiration for similar projects. Finally, this book does such an insightful job of balancing 'the duty of care vs. the dignity of risk' that us caregivers face all the time. Wish the book was longer!"

Dan Strauss, *father of an autistic son*

"*Neuro-Inclusive Community Design* inspires me to consider more ways in which our planned cohousing village might fully include individuals with developmental disabilities. It's like three books in one: it's certainly a respectful history of one amazing inclusive community in Iceland, Sólheimar Ecovillage. It's also a collection of testimonials from the special – and privileged – residents there. Third, the hundreds of photographs throughout the book are a catalog of life there, showing me life in cohousing – the rooms people live in, the gardens they grow, the crafts and other projects that make life meaningful for the residents.

We started planning our project with the idea of creating a place for our 28-year-old daughter to live near us but in her own cottage or apartment. Now we're considering inviting other families we know who similarly have an adult child with disabilities to pitch in with us. I'll recommend this book to them."

Daniel Stusser, *Jolt Newspaper owner, parent of two adult children with autism*

"In *Neuro-Inclusive Community Design* Durrett inspires us to create loving and nurturing village communities designed to be neuro-inclusive. Supportive informal village environments connected by foot to nature, farm and community, operating at a rhythm in sync with the resident's needs with supportive community at its heart. Durrett, with his extensive cohousing community background, walks us through the areas to focus on and the pitfalls to avoid in the context of the amazing historic Sólheimar Ecovillage in Iceland. An illuminating book that exposes the inadequacy of independence/isolation and institutions, revealing the craft and humanity of creating supportive village communities."

Greg Ramsey, *Architect, Land Use Consultant*

"The author, Charles Durrett, who has written many books about cohousing communities, takes his advocacy and knowledge in new directions to impart new knowledge about community living with support systems in place for neurodivergent people. This important book documents what has worked well for housing and caring for people who are neurodivergent, most typically, those with autism and those with Down syndrome, in the Sólheimer Ecovillage in Iceland.

The guiding principle of Sólheimer is that 'Quality-of-life amenities that make life more comfortable, more fun, more convenient, more fulfilling, and more meaningful are the results of purposeful work.' Purposeful work also has the added benefit of encouraging social engagement and resulting relationships. Sólheimer provides several choices for purposeful work and opportunities for residents to be together, including artisanal handicrafts, greenhouse food production, and participation in theatrical productions.

A professionally trained staff supports the residents by treating them with respect, identifying what they want and need, and how best to provide this support. The staff addresses 'not only basic needs but also emotional and social needs.' Because Sólheimer is an ecovillage, the staff live there, among the residents they care for.

Charles Durrett also investigates the financial burden and emotional impact on US families that have neurodivergent members, and the lack of meaningful alternatives for their care. The ground-breaking ideas in this significant book offer a meaningful alternative for caring for the neurodivergent members of our society."

David Burwen, *Senior Cohousing Developer*

"I thoroughly enjoyed this wonderful book where the author Charles Durrett goes into great detail on this amazing 94-year-old village in Iceland where individuals with Down syndrome and autism find an amazing home and workplace. From the interesting history of the community to the ecovillage of today, this book takes an in-depth look at what a neuro-inclusive community means to residents for productivity, pride and purpose, and includes a discussion on the existing architecture and suggestions for improvement to make it even more valuable. Daily life is portrayed with such lovely detail on staff and volunteer interaction with residents as friends, and the economics and management of the village are so helpful in understanding how someone might begin to translate this type of community in other places. I love the statement that 'No one is being warehoused here'. I plan to pass this on to the mother of a young adult son with autism, and my hope is that because of this beautiful book perhaps many more folks with these conditions will be able to realize their one life and live it to the fullest."

Sue Smith, *Senior Cohousing Resident*

"Charles Durrett's *Neuro-Inclusive Community Design* delivers an insightful, practical, and heartwarming exploration of the power of community, specifically designed for individuals with intellectual and developmental disabilities (I/DD). Through the lens of Iceland's Sólheimar Ecovillage, this book presents an extraordinary blueprint for creating environments where everyone can not only live but thrive.

What truly makes this book invaluable is its clear focus on showing how cohousing provides an innovative alternative to the more conventional and often limiting systems for people with I/DD. It illustrates how community-building, love, and intentional infrastructure design can dramatically enhance the quality of life for individuals typically labeled as marginalized or dependent. From gardening and arts to everyday tasks like cooking and cleaning, the residents of Sólheimar prove that meaningful contributions are possible for all when given the right environment.

The storytelling is as moving as it is practical. Durrett paints a vivid picture of how the Sólheimar community came to life and he walks us through the crucial steps in setting up a similar system anywhere. This is a game-changing resource for anyone looking to build something far more fulfilling and humanizing than the current options available.

If you're designing or envisioning a future where folks with I/DD can flourish in society, this book is a must-read. Its combination of real-world examples, strategic insights, and inspiring human stories will leave you not only informed but deeply motivated to take action."

Chris Ortiz, *Special Needs Cohousing Developer*

"How this community (that Chuck describes so well) goes about honoring, supporting and operating to meet each other's needs is the type of community I want to help create and live in. Chuck's writing and the photos in the book are very inspiring to me. My hope is that more people read and share this book with others, and start to make intentional communities like this that will meet their needs and the needs of those they care about. If you are interested at all at doing this type of thing for yourself and others, I highly recommend buying this book and reading the other books written by Chuck Durrett about cohousing."

Mike Swettenam, *Cohousing Co-Creator, teacher of many students with autism*

"Charles has written the masterclass on expanding diversity in community. He paints a clear picture of forming community through collaboration. Essential reading for those looking to do the same."

David Leeke, *Reader*

"This is an amazing book that hit me right in the heart! Chuck's descriptions, both physically and emotionally, of this beautiful ecovillage in Iceland resonated strongly with me. I am familiar with intentional communities in Canada and am in the process of becoming part of one in Langley, BC. I have a daughter who would benefit from support as she moves through her life. Chuck's words and the vision he presents have ignited a desire in me to help shape the culture I will be living in. It has helped me clarify that our community needs to serve all of our members excellently, including creating room and love for my daughter, so that she can thrive in her own particular way. Thank you, Chuck!"

John Frederickson, *Teacher*

"I have several friends who have children on the spectrum of autism. Many of them are looking at the very issues that this book addresses so clearly: How will my children cope with housing and many other social problems when I have died? Charles Durrett in this terrific book describes the creation and ongoing growth of a marvelous community in Iceland that embraces this group of people.

I am fortunate to live in a town that has two co-housing communities. To extend this model as a foundation for housing and supporting people of all ages with neurological challenges is a brilliant concept. And this community in Iceland shows just how well it works. Bravo!"

Brian Gibb, *Financial Advisor*

"I live in a cohousing community. This book about Sólheimar Ecovillage reminds me of, and reinforces, ideals that drove my participation in community 30 years ago. More importantly, this book provides clear and practical evidence of the health benefits of creating an intentionally interactive web of relationships. My goal is to support my neighbors' and my own passions, and to be able to look deeply at ways that I and We can improve our connections and our health. What I read so eagerly for in this book were nuggets of simple wisdom that give me the juice of inspiration. Frankly, this is an easy and fun read, not at all like a textbook from my distant memory. I can tell from the storytelling that the author is coming from a place of lived experience and genuine curiosity about how physical spaces inform social interaction and how people (occupiers of space) inform the design. It's a profound symbiosis when done well. I am not trying to create a new community. However, 30 years in, my community is more than a generation into our evolution. We are experiencing aging differently, we have had a turnover of 2/3 of the original residents, and we have discovered opportunities and challenges that we didn't actively plan for. This book leans on the history and current events of one amazing community to give me (and any reader) inspiration to do good work in our own place in the world."

Scott Bird, *Cohousing Co-developer*

"*Neuro-Inclusive Community Design* by Charles Durrett reveals how an Icelandic neurodiverse intentional community steeped in kindness, respect, and interdependence can positively impact the lives of individuals with intellectual and developmental disabilities (IDD). As a parent of a daughter with an IDD, this was not surprising. But what was especially moving and inspiring was reading the accounts from community residents who don't experience disability, and how their lives were transformed and enriched as a result of living alongside those with varying abilities.

Neuro-Inclusive Community Design takes the reader on a beautiful journey through the Sólheimar Ecovillage. It was founded in 1930 by a visionary, a young woman passionate about caring for vulnerable children and those with disabilities. Although Sólheimar has evolved and changed in its physical layout over the past 94 years, what hasn't changed are its guiding principles and philosophy, and the belief that everyone deserves a life of purpose and is capable of contributing to society.

The book covers all aspects of this community. We meet community members, learn about the importance of design when creating spaces for organic interactions, and what the financial needs are to sustain such a community. We are taken on a tour via text and images through the variety of on-campus 'workshops' where residents can make functional objects and create art, fix things, care for plants and gardens, and cook. One chapter also speaks to the special care of elderly residents.

Towards the end of the book, Durrett explores how a cohousing community might serve the needs of those with IDD while embracing the philosophy of Sólheimar. He provides a step-by-step guide for those who are moved to create a neuro-inclusive cohousing community. While I embrace the concept of cohousing and intentional communities, the reality of funding such projects and making them affordable to those with IDD is a great challenge in the United States, especially when considering locations that are close to resources and amenities. Yet, that shouldn't be a deterrent from following one's dream. Thank you, Mr. Durrett for highlighting a population that is often overlooked and marginalized, and for telling such a beautiful and moving story.

This book is for anyone who dreams of creating a community where all community members are embraced and celebrated for their differences, or anyone who is looking for an inspirational read about our shared humanity."

Beate Sass, *parent of a daughter with IDD*

"As the director of a non-profit that develops housing co-ops, I found this book very insightful, informative and inspiring! I have known many families who face enormous difficulties finding suitable housing for their adult children with various intellectual or developmental disabilities. Charles Durrett, using the example of one inspiring community along with short descriptions of several others, shows how it can be done in a way that improves lives, affirms human dignity and reduces social costs. This book is a very valuable resource for the housing world in general, and especially for those working to improve the lives of those who are neurologically challenged."

Dan Bryant, *Director of Affordable Housing Non-profit*

"I was deeply moved by Charles Durrett's refreshingly hopeful new book "*Neuro-Inclusive Community Design*". Durrett records through copious details and touching personal voices the inner life of the Sólheimar community, revealing how an undervalued community can offer secrets to a whole and fulfilling way of living."

Jeffrey Reed, *Artist*

"The social, financial and environmental benefits of co-housing communities for folks of many different stripes has long been understood. Here, the author takes co-housing principles a huge leap forward, with a detailed and uplifting case study of a community dedicated to the well-being of adults with Down syndrome, autism and other neuro-diagnoses. It is an inspiring work, even for someone who does not have significant, first-hand experience with neurodiverse individuals. For people like a friend of mine, who has a teenage son with moderate autism and is contemplating the child's future, this book will be a godsend. I can't wait to send her a copy!"

Lee Auerbach, *Lawyer*

"I liked that the thing we all are susceptible to – loneliness – is addressed head-on as a prime motivation for co-housing communities, for all people, not just those with special needs. For those with special needs, their families' concerns for them as their parents/caregivers get older, this is a superior option. Thank you Charles for your visionary work!"

R. Viola, *Reader*

"Incredible read and great visuals. This book brings to reality what's possible. It was like visiting the community first hand. Great ideas for life in general too."

Geneva Bigelow, *Social Activist*

"As an 82-year-old man with Parkinson's, I very much appreciated receiving a copy of *Neuro-Inclusive Community Design* as a gift on my recent birthday. Charles Durrett, the author, explains how it is possible to create neuro-inclusive communities in the context of cohousing to make life more manageable and meaningful for people dealing with neurological and intellectual disorders — from youngsters with autism, Down syndrome or other ailments, to old geezers like me who no longer walk with authority nor are able to maintain a level of balance, strength or mobility that most folks take for granted.

Although the book centers on the accomplishments of Sólheimar Ecovillage in Iceland, the need for similar housing accommodations and amenities is as universal as the plethora of mental and physical issues that impact millions of people of all ages and cultures around the world. It is very much a book about the limitless power of community.

Mr. Durrett demonstrates that for every challenge there is a solution, and passionately addresses the core goals for neurologically and intellectually challenged individuals—young and old—to live lives of productivity, pride and purpose. As a former professional athlete who now labors to walk our dog, stroll a hundred feet to the mailbox, or open a child-proof medicine bottle, the idea of living in the kind of supportive community described in the book is very appealing.

I strongly recommend the liberally illustrated, thoughtfully written and highly inspirational *Neuro-Inclusive Community Design*, and look forward to a neuro-inclusive community emerging soon here in Northeast Florida."

Steve Cottrell, *Mayor and Political Advocate for a built cohousing community*

NEURO-INCLUSIVE COMMUNITY DESIGN

This book is an inspiring exploration of Sólheimar Ecovillage in Iceland, a pioneering community that embodies sustainability, social responsibility, and inclusivity.

Cohousing expert Charles Durrett delves into the unique aspects of this ecovillage of about 100 residents, 45 of whom include those with developmental and intellectual disabilities, who live and thrive alongside neighbors in a safe and enriching environment. Through rich storytelling and detailed first-person accounts, the book highlights the importance of creating communities that celebrate and support neurodiversity. Durrett presents Sólheimar as a model for how we can build neuro-inclusive spaces that respect and uplift every individual's potential, fostering a sense of belonging and purpose. The book offers practical insights into the design, the principles, and the practices that make Sólheimar a standout community for inclusive living. It challenges readers to rethink conventional approaches, advocating for environments where all people, regardless of their cognitive differences, can live meaningful and fulfilling lives. Durrett also presents case studies of four other neuro-inclusive communities, including Hertha Levefallesskab, WeBUILT (We Build Unique Independent Lives Together), Creative Living Community of CT, and L'Arche International Movement. With its focus on real-world solutions and its call to action, this book is both a guide and an inspiration for anyone interested in the intersection of sustainability, community living, and neuro-inclusivity.

It will have a broad audience of architects, designers, occupational therapists, mental health professionals, housing developers, and practitioners in housing and social care, among others.

Charles Durrett is an architect and author based in California. With Kathryn McCamant, Charles introduced the concept of cohousing to the United States with the seminal book *Cohousing: A Contemporary Approach to Housing Ourselves*. Durrett and his team at The Cohousing Company have designed more than 55 cohousing communities in the United States and around the world. His work has been featured in *Time Magazine, The New York Times, The Los Angeles Times, The San Francisco Chronicle, The Guardian, Architecture, The Wall Street Journal, The Economist*, and many other publications.

NEURO-INCLUSIVE COMMUNITY DESIGN

Lessons from Sólheimar Ecovillage

Second Edition

Charles Durrett

Routledge
Taylor & Francis Group
LONDON AND NEW YORK

Designed cover image: Visit South Iceland

Second edition published 2026
by Routledge
4 Park Square, Milton Park, Abingdon, Oxon OX14 4RN

and by Routledge
605 Third Avenue, New York, NY 10158

Routledge is an imprint of the Taylor & Francis Group, an informa business

First edition published as 'One Life, Live It: Sólheimar Ecovillage and the Importance of Neuro-Inclusive Communities' by The Cohousing Company 2024

British Library Cataloguing-in-Publication Data
A catalogue record for this book is available from the British Library

ISBN: 978-1-041-07820-3 (hbk)
ISBN: 978-1-041-07819-7 (pbk)
ISBN: 978-1-003-64233-6 (ebk)

DOI: 10.4324/9781003642336

Typeset in Times New Roman
by Apex CoVantage, LLC

To Sesselja Sigmundsdóttir.
With vision, compassion, tenacity, and diligence, she
built this beacon in this place. Her work, Sólheimar, is inspiring the residents to be their
best selves and reach their potential—shining the light to guide all of our lives.

The community of Sólheimar is inspiring the world to reimagine best practices
when it comes to setting neurodiverse folks up for success.

TABLE OF CONTENTS

ACKNOWLEDGMENTS

The help I received from others is infinite. I want to thank all the residents, or as they call themselves locally, the "Home People." They are not patients nor clients—they are the friends and neighbors of each other and of those whom we would normally characterize as caregivers and sociologists. They are clearly contributors to their neighborhood, from "The Big Play" to the choir, to the daily well-being of others, and to the arts, crafts, industriousness, maintenance, and the GDP of Iceland. They carry their weight; they bring meaning to their place. Nobody is being warehoused here, thanks to everyone involved.

Thanks to the moms and dads, brothers and sisters, who cared enough to ensure that their loved one was hanging out somewhere where they could be somebody, where neighbors know, care for, and support each other. Thanks to the relatives who wanted their loved one to have a whole life. And to the city, county, and national Icelandic governments and foundations like the *Blue Lagoon* and the *Lions Club* that help support Sólheimar. You seek and support a civilized and viable society and work toward that end.

Thanks to the Board of Directors of Sólheimar, who volunteered their time to help manage the plethora of details from the new handicap ramps to balancing the budget. Thanks to The Chairman of the Board, *Sigurjón Örn Pórsson*, and those who find the money when it's needed and best assure that the ledger balances.

Crucial are the Staff and Friends at Sólheimar—those that help set the community up for day-to-day success and also helped set this book up for success:

Anna Þuríður Pálsdóttir; *Hallbjörn (Halli Valli) Rúnarsson*; *Valgeir Fridolf Backman; Eiður Eyþórsson* (forestry); *Ina Kjartansdóttir* (greenhouse); *Elfa Bjork Kristjansdottir*; *Dagny Davidsdottir*; and many others who helped in big and small ways.

Workshop teachers who helped with explanations and translations, residents who spoke English that helped translate, and social workers who helped with translations as well.

And thank you to the folks working at The Cohousing Company, especially *Nadthachai Kongkhajornkidsuk*; *Yisha Liu* and *Aidan Kurtz*, who came in as interns and plugged in right away; *Laurenne Ross*, another intern who helped with her unique editing skills that made this book more readable and gave it “flow”; and *Bethany Celio* who came in as a private contractor to help us get this important story told.

The nexus of community and quality of life could not have been communicated as well without the help of the following manuscript reviewers:

Dr. Søren Erik Skovlund (Senior Director, Patient Engagement and Patient-Centered Research Science); *Dr. Jeffrey Conklin* psychologist, PhD (with many diagnosed patients); *Laura Juvik* (Danish Architect and Board Member on the Danish Cohousing Association); *Dr. Bill Thomas* (Founder and Chairman at Minka); *Cam Doré* (Former Director of Burnaby Association for the Mentally Handicapped, Gentle Teaching Expert); *Desiree Kameka Galloway* (Lead Consultant of Neuro-Inclusive Housing Solutions and Director of Autism Housing Networks); *Paul Platner* (Guardian of Child with Down syndrome, founder of EnGaged Services and Special Needs Advocates); *Irene Masteller* (Grandmother and activist with autistic Grandchild); Alexandria Levitt (USC, MS); *Janet Palmer* (Cohousing Expert) for help with Chapter 5 (Blaskogar); *Jack Salmon* (Cohousing Enthusiast and Author); *Joy Hertz* (Aspiring News Diverse Community Developer); *Jeanne Dickenson* (A True Communitarian); *Marty Maskall* (Editing); *Rory Kuczek* (Sólheimar Volunteer whose paragraphs and essays were written for this book) and *Karen Hamilton* (who I have heard espouse how work and purpose feeds the soul since I was 15 years old—and still do from time to time). I so respect these good people and their contributions to this effort.

ABOUT THE AUTHOR

Charles R. Durrett, AIA, is an architect, author, and advocate of affordable, socially responsible, sustainable design and diverse housing to serve a variety of populations. He has made major contributions to community-based architecture and cohousing. For a comprehensive understanding of cohousing communities, see Charles' recent work, *Cohousing Communities: Designing for High-Functioning Neighborhoods,* published by Wiley & Sons; his other books include *The Senior Cohousing Handbook: A Community Approach to Independent Living,* as well as 14 other books about housing, including *A Solution to Homelessness in Your Town.*

Charles Durrett is credited in the Oxford English Dictionary for coining the word: Cohousing.

Charles has designed over 55 cohousing communities in North America, including the first Cohousing project in Davis, California, in 1989, and has consulted on many more around the world.

Charles and his team of architects have also designed an equal number of affordable housing projects and schools. His work has been featured in *Time Magazine, The New York Times, The LA Times, The San Francisco Chronicle, The Boston Globe, The Washington Post, The Guardian, Architecture, Architectural Record, The Wall Street Journal, The Economist,* and many more. Charles has also been a guest on a wide variety of televised talk shows, such as *The Today Show,* and a wide variety of other news programs, including *CNN, The McNeil Lehr Report,* and others.

He has received numerous awards, which include the *World Habitat Award* presented by The United Nations, the *Silver Achievement Award for Active Adult Community* by the National Association of Home Builders (NAHB) 50+ Housing Council, the *Silver Energy Value Housing Award* by NAHB, the *Mixed Use/Mixed Income Development Award* presented jointly by the

American Institute of Architects and the United States Department of Housing and Urban Development and is a recipient of the *Global Over 50's Housing/Healthcare Award*. He was also declared a *Visionary of the Sierras* by the *Sierra Business Council* for his new cohousing communities in Nevada City and Grass Valley, California, and *The Institute of Special Innovations*, London, England *Innovator of the Year* award in 1989.

His many public presentations include two to the United States Congress about affordable housing and to *The Commonwealth Club of California*. He has given dozens of presentations for housing conferences and professional organizations, such as the American Institute of Architects, and scores of presentations to universities, including Princeton; Stanford; U.C. Berkeley; University of Oregon, University of Wisconsin-Milwaukee; University of Minnesota; Oklahoma State University; and the largest architecture school in the U.S. and his alma mater, California Polytechnic University. The Royal Danish University, School of Architecture, The University of Lund in Sweden; The Art and Architecture Institute of Iceland in Reykjavik; Simon Fraser in Canada; a dozen universities in Germany and many more.

Charles Durrett continues to devote his time to new and diverse community-orientated housing projects and start-ups. As an architect, he realized long ago that developing healthy environments requires starting with the culture and seeking a much wider array of issues than just the sticks and bricks.

He lives in a 34-unit cohousing community, Nevada City Cohousing in Northern California, which he designed with the future residents in 2004.

Charles recently had the honor of personally presenting this book to Guðni Thorlacius Jóhannesson, the President of Iceland, and was proud to do so. President Jóhannesson is highly motivated to leverage this book to develop new cohousing communities for the neurodivergent population.

LIST OF FIGURE CREDITS

Figure 1.1 Solheimar History Museum
Figure 1.2 Solheimar History Museum
Figure 1.3 Solheimar History Museum
Figure 1.4 Solheimar History Museum
Figure 1.8 Solheimar History Museum
Figure 1.9 Solheimar History Museum
Figure 1.10 Solheimar History Museum
Figure 1.11 Solheimar History Museum
Figure 2.26 Chris Samuel
Figure 3.24 Markaðsstofa Suðurlands
Figure 3.48 Markaðsstofa Suðurlands
Figure 3.49 Markaðsstofa Suðurlands
Figure 3.64 Markaðsstofa Suðurlands
Figure 7.5 World Wide Friends
Figure 9.7 WeBUILT
Figure 9.8 WeBUILT
Figure 9.9 WeBUILT
Figure 9.10 Union Studio Architecture and Community Design
Figure 9.11 Union Studio Architecture and Community Design
Figure 9.12 Creative Living
Figure 9.13 Creative Living
Figure 9.14 L'Arche Jacksonville
Figure 9.15 L'Arche Jacksonville

FOREWORD

I've never been a political person. Sitting in a stuffy, windowless, Washington DC ballroom, I was at the annual conference of our nation's care system because federal Medicaid officials had just declared that "intentional communities" were "presumptively institutional." With this one small regulatory interpretation, the lifeline of publicly-funded support services for thousands of adults with Intellectual/Developmental Disabilities (I/DD) was suddenly at risk if they chose to live together in any disability-specific farmstead, gated community, residential school, or campus.

Patch Adams delivered the heartfelt keynote. As a world traveler, he described the medical power of smiles and laughter, interdependence in relationships, and knowing what people prefer in their tea. Believing he had softened their concrete thinking, I stood up and asked, "Do you think intentional communities are a good option to support people with disabilities?" He stared at me blankly and responded with a resounding, "Duh!" At that moment, the glare of 1,000 eyes turned towards me as I just questioned the sacred cow of "independent living." I was called a neo-institutionalist.

Past sins of institutionalization—where scores of people with disabilities were involuntarily segregated and warehoused in large impersonal buildings—catalyzed the inclusion movement decades ago. This movement was, and still is, life-changing. Simultaneously, it quietly fed an ableist ideology that neurotypical classmates, coworkers, and neighbors are better than disabled ones. U.S. policy is driven by this limited interpretation of "community integration," which is more easily defined by geography and the density of persons with disabilities than what one may find in the heartbeat of an intentional community.

What Is the Cost of Doing Nothing?

Taylor was found walking down the highway of the rural community where we live; the family he was sent to live with could no longer support him. His options beyond homelessness were to be displaced into a group home or adult foster care. Taylor is autistic, 6'2", 200 pounds with a full beard, a person of faith, and a generous spirit. Seated around the beautiful table Taylor graciously made us as a woodworking apprentice, we decided he would move in with us until something better came along.

During the two years Taylor lived with us, we spent many nights laughing around that table. Every day was an opportunity to discuss little life lessons: the thin line between just friendship and flirting with potential girlfriends (including how to put a hat on a banana); what to do if approached by the police (share loudly that he is autistic with his hands over his head); or sticking to a budget during quiet, uncrowded night time grocery runs (not spending $60 on ¼ inch thick slices of London broil for steak sandwiches!).

Eventually, Taylor moved out and became a "success" story. He lives in his government-subsidized apartment, has "competitive, integrated employment," and has access to Medicaid-funded staff to help him stay independent. Not too long ago, he called and told me that he was temporarily admitted to the psychiatric hospital and hoping to go back as he met some friends there. In his integrated apartment, Taylor is surrounded by people yet is desperate for relationships.

In my research on neuro-inclusive community development, over 85% of the neurodivergent population report feeling lonely, and the majority do not have any close friends.

Upending Over-Rated Independence

Now, ten years after that conference in D.C., a tsunami of change is building. Loud self-advocate and family voices are being heard: forced integration is as dehumanizing as forced segregation. The research I started years ago is providing the data that shows people want to live in planned communities and cohousing—and I learn of new emerging developments nearly every week! Federal Medicaid officials have rescinded their previous guidance about classifying intentional communities as presumptively institutional. "Even well-intentioned policies from Washington often lack the flexibility needed to work for every state, community, setting, or family," said Medicaid Administrator Seema Verma.

Banding together with others to develop neuro-inclusive cohousing will provide not only future housing stability but also a safety net of neurodiverse relationships that are just a knock away. We can choose to make our greatest financial investment (housing) in neighborhoods that heal people from what the U.S. Surgeon General has declared an epidemic of loneliness sweeping through the population.

Living in an intentional community is invaluable preventative medicine against isolation, neglect, and abuse. People will notice if you didn't make it to Taco Tuesday in the Common House or ask about your new friend during the Sunday morning walking group.

Sólheimar Ecovillage and the communities in the pages that follow are built on the values of connectedness, relationships, self-direction, and creativity of adults with I/DD in spaces designed to be physically, cognitively, and relationally accessible. These examples shed light on an alternative model: interdependent living.

There Is No Time to Wait

To the changemakers across the country: gather together. Learn from each other's mistakes. Support one another. We can prevent the trauma of displacement or homelessness of adults with I/DD and pave diverse paths to meaningful community life.

We can no longer afford to bear the cost of doing nothing. May the pages of this book fuel the fire in your heart to change the status quo and create something extraordinary.

Desiree Kameka Galloway

Director, Autism Housing Network
Lead Consultant, Neuro-Inclusive Housing Solutions

INTRODUCTION

I worry about my child when I'm gone. He's 37 now. He needs a community where others know him, care about him, and support him. He wants purpose—he wants to fit in with others, and to get "traction" in life—to have friends and to visit like everyone else.

—Mom

Iceland's Sólheimar Ecovillage and other like-communities around the world have proven that folks with autism, Down syndrome, and other neurological challenges can and do thrive in a community. Sólheimar has irrefutably demonstrated, without a doubt, that "One Life, Live It!" is achievable for all.

Reaching Our Potential

This community was designed to set people with intellectual disabilities and neurological challenges up for success. Sólheimar has helped over 1,000 people with compromised neurological systems reach their personal potential. All that the residents want here is a place to have purpose and to be useful, to experience a social life, to be appreciated, widely respected, engaged, and accepted—even to prosper. When all is said and done, they have all of that and more.

Living Our Best Lives in Community

While a commitment to sustainability is integral to the mission of Sólheimar, the empowering nature of the community proves to be the most sustainable aspect of this remarkable project. The belief underlying the village's mission and operations is that each and every person, no matter what the challenges they face, can make valuable contributions to the community—and it works. Together, they garden, manage and keep up the facilities, work in the cafe, bakery, and store, put on plays, and make considerable for-sale crafts. They shop for groceries, and they cook and clean. Sólheimar welcomes people who have been all too often labeled as helpless and/or hopeless and are relegated to the margins of society. Here, they are provided with and co-create a community in which they can have meaningful participation and maintain agency over their days and their lives.

DOI: 10.4324/9781003642336-1

A Fair Chance

> *The heart of Sólheimar ideology is the same as it was in July 1930: to give individuals a fair chance and maximize the potential of every person. Sólheimar creates the space and opportunities for each person to grow and develop, thus becoming an important and active participant in the community. Each person is unique with their own abilities, their own development, and their own talents. We always look at the opportunities that live within each person, not the limitations.*
>
> *—Sólheimar mission*

Each Doing Our Part

The notion is that residents benefit from these shared environments and that community—and a sense of pride and ownership—are developed. If one person knows how to use the bus or can be adequately trained to do so, that person will help and teach others. One person can shop, a couple of people can cook, and a couple of people can clean. The need for caregivers and outside supervision is reduced because everyone works as a team. The operative concept is that with this division of labor and communal spirit, anything is possible.

We know we're better off with cooperation . . . isn't that true for all of us? Life in Sólheimar is organized around this idea of cooperation and emotional co-ownership. Not only does this provide structure, but it also provides a much more affordable framework and ways of living that are better than having folks live isolated at home or in an institutional setting. What ensues is engagement, purpose, independence, self-acceptance, and others to commune with every day.

For so many reasons, Sólheimar is a haven. The community and love here are palpable. The staff and "clients" refer to each other as "friends" and say that "we are all equal" as a common refrain. It may seem like a small detail, but the semantics ("friends") and gentle teaching methodologies utilized are truly making tangible differences. Starting with the 100 inhabitants, everyone teaches

Common lunch. "I want to have lunch with so and so—we haven't talked in a week." "This is the textile art workshop crew; I want to hear about their new projects . . ." and so on. This may not seem profound at first—this is simply "One Life, Live It!" But these little joys in life compound, and you realize they actually are the currency of a positive, pro-social life. They enable a place and a life where every person is intentionally and perceptibly accepted.

Common dining brings the entire community together each day. This is not just physiological sustenance; this is emotional sustenance. Catching up with each other, "What are you doing this weekend?", "How are you doing?" and so on.

This is where the magic happens. "How are you, and you, and how are you?" as Louis Armstrong says, what they are really saying is, "I love you."

one another who, along with their families, are motivated to create for themselves a better, more fulfilling life. The social workers here invoke love and appreciation for others readily and predictably. The entire ensemble—physical, social, emotional—allows an optimized environment for everyone. They have clearly embraced the notion that we are all friends and we are all equal.

Islands of Acceptance, Engagement, and Appreciation

Some argue that when the world falls apart, the only thing that can save us is a strong, functioning, local community. But for many, the world has already fallen apart. There's nothing like a chromosomal abnormality to create neurological havoc and throw your life into chaos from the onset. Historically, too many of these folks have been cast adrift and lost. Their hopes and dreams are lost along with meaningful existence, especially when all they want is to have what others have: to be accepted, to have purpose, and to reach their potential. Places like Sólheimar, however, are islands of acceptance, engagement, and true appreciation. Here, they have found a refuge.

Inspiration, Vision, Actualization

If we only accomplish one thing in this book, we want to show you how doable creating a community like Sólheimar is. We will dive into the details as we go on, but everything that really matters is here in this book. Our obvious beginning lies with Sesselja Sigmundsdóttir, the initiator of Sólheimar. She led with heart and the frame of mind that "it is possible, we can do it, and it's worth it." In the U.S. and elsewhere, the funding scenarios clearly must be addressed; they had to resolve funding at Sólheimar as well, and they started doing so before government funding existed. The only thing stopping us is a vision and a deliberate process. The actualization of a community such as this one will only happen when inspired individuals take the lead. We can learn so much from Sesselja's visionary work, legacy, and the proven success of Sólheimar.

This is why it's important to do the design process with the future residents. The design will be much richer and more appropriate, and they will own it. This is an ownership that will be passed on for many generations.

Here I am enjoying common lunch with Sólheimar residents. When I paid attention, close attention, I had insights into their lives and into my own that I will never forget: insights about neurodiversity that I would never discover on my own or with others who don't have a neurodiverse take on life. They're the kind of insights that were more enlightening to me than conversations with experts. To swim with these folks is like scuba diving in a sea chock full of tropical fish around and through the coral. This is the setting where I repeatedly learned the most.

Nexus between Community and Quality of Life

There is a nexus between community and quality of life for folks with autism, Down syndrome, and other neurodiversity challenges. Providing more efficient care saves families and governments money, making more and better care possible. This efficiency of care is important, but it is not sufficient. Our goal should be to create and nurture a sense of community that produces smiles, joy, and happiness among its members and advances affordability as well. The poster in our office says, "If it doesn't work socially, why bother?"

What difference does acceptance, respect, inclusion, kinship, and purpose make? Well-considered living environments can give "patients" more than good housing.

A sense of community grows by giving people a stake and a participatory role, connecting them through social context. Raking the grass, washing windows, tending a garden, and building shelves—together—builds satisfaction and pride.

Demanding Better Working Models Proven by Experience

This book is about saving the families of neurodivergent people money, as affording "care" can be an immense challenge for them. It is also, in theory, about saving governments money. But it's primarily about facing the fact that many governments are not likely to ever adequately fund this kind of care. So, how are we going to get adequate care provided?

This is not an academic study; Sólheimar and other similar communities have given us working models proven by *experience*. What is needed now is a movement to expand and improve care based on those models. This book attempts to help families consider alternatives to institutions or "home alone." Parents will be the ones to say, "Together, in partnership with our families, our government, the industriousness of the residents themselves, and with participating non-profits, we can reach the potential of "One Life, Live It!"

"One Life, Live It!"

Build and sustain your community: not via media, but via one real face-to-face conversation at a time and real problem-solving along the way.

Casual time.

Everyday face-to-face, heart-to-heart connection is beautiful. Building and maintaining relationships, imparting information, discussing the issues of the day, lamenting, and celebrating the meaning of life are all important components of fulfillment.

Making a Viable Society Through Village Life

The possibility for each individual to realize their own potential lies in the making of a more viable village society—even if it is only a very proximate one. In fact, it's only the proximate one that can: the village of known people where you feel safe, where you can walk and readily talk to one another. This is not nuclear science; it is so basic that we often forget. These behaviors are observable, and their worth is palpable; they are the difference between an unfulfilled life and a fulfilled life.

A Practical Guide

This book strives to illustrate the immense accomplishments of Sólheimar so that the reader can get inspired. The intent of this book is clear—to encourage, support, and enable the reader to take action and make change happen through the application of community and cohousing principles. Each community is unique and has its own path. While Sólheimar is a unique community, the world is on the precipice of recognizing the value of community based on accepted therapeutic principles. In *Cohousing: A Contemporary Approach to Housing Ourselves*, my first book with Kathryn McCamant, we introduced cohousing to North America. It is a lifestyle story. My earlier books about cohousing in Denmark have been inspiring Americans; about 150 cohousing communities have been built (as of 2024) since the first book was published in July 1988. Time Magazine predicted in 1992 that there would be 200 built by 2020. We hope that hundreds of Sólheimars will be built in North America by 2050.

Sólheimar has come up with a tried-and-true formula for all of us to learn from. Go forth, see what they have done, see what you can do to give others a healthy life, and realize, "One Life, Live It!"

If you ever experience art done by folks with autism, they are often nothing less than profound.

Gathering in front of the common house—true village life—keeps people connected.

Sólheimar holds one common meeting every morning where common issues are discussed. For example, "We have an American visitor this week, and he will be taking photos."

CHAPTER 1

I'll find a way . . .
. . . focus on possibilities,
not limitations.

-Sesselja Hreindís Sigmundsdóttir

How Sólheimar Was Started

This chapter is based on the biography of Sesselja, "Mér leggst eitthvað til: sagan af Sesselju Sigmundsdóttur og Sólheimum" (translated to: I Have Something in Mind: The Story of Sesselja Sigmundsdóttir and Sólheimar)—written in 1990 by Jónina Michaelsdóttir and Sessljа's brother Þórarinn—as well as the historic record at Sólheimahús, the first home where Sesselja and the orphaned children lived which now acts as a historical museum in the ecovillage honoring the history of Sólheimar.

Sólheimar's beginnings provide a long and fascinating tale. This storied history does not, however, imply that new project leaders need to suffer like Sesselja Sigmundsdóttir (founder of Sólheimar) did to get their projects built. Sólheimar was started in 1930, and while the world has extolled the success of this project, no more of them have been built in Iceland to date. This is a story about how a project can become a *model* project, not through blood, sweat, and tears, but through determination, love, and an extremely deliberate process. Sesselja's work has shown us not how to suffer—she did that for us, but how important the community is to folks who need others but can't easily reach out. It is a guide to wellbeing, quality of life, attaining purpose, and to teaching us how to live life to the fullest.

Sesselja encountered many obstacles that we can avoid—*we just have to make the process a deliberate one*. We need a process that cuts out most of the trials and errors, and we now have one. New efforts can shoot for the end goal: healthy relationships—even kinship—in a village-like setting that saves governments and families money, creates real security, relieves parental burdens, helps siblings, and does so much more.

DOI: 10.4324/9781003642336-2

Sesselja Sigmundsdóttir and the children of Sólheimar.

Sesselja Hreindís Sigmundsdóttir: Nature Lover and Humanitarian

Over recent centuries, Iceland has produced a host of astonishing women who have achieved great things, mostly because they followed their hearts to manifest their dreams. Among that group, Sesselja Sigmundsdóttir is a first among equals. Sesselja is remembered as a lover of nature and a humanitarian with a strong sense of justice. She had a natural predisposition to care for the vulnerable, and to them, she devoted her life's work. Sesselja was a religious woman, but she worshiped the human potential as much as her own faith.

Training and Development (Rudolf Steiner's Philosophy)

Following her passion and conviction to serve the less fortunate, Sesselja moved to Denmark in 1923 and later to Switzerland and Germany to study the subjects of pedagogy and pediatric nursing; she was the first Icelander to train in care for people with developmental disabilities.

During her time in Germany, Sesselja had the opportunity to attend a school's convention in Hamburg in 1928, where she met a group of pupils from the Waldorf School in Stuttgart. Their work was based on the anthroposophical teachings of Dr. Rudolf Steiner (1861–1925). She was especially drawn to Steiner's ideas about pedagogy, health, education, and horticulture, as she saw how they impacted children and increased their patience, focus, self-confidence, and "windows of tolerance."

Sesselja also had the opportunity to study gardening, floriculture, and animal farming practices; she incorporated all of her diverse studies and her passion for social justice to create the ecovillage ***Sólheimar—Home of the Sun***.

Children's Home Committee and Hverakot

Around the time that her study abroad was coming to an end, Sesselja had a chance to speak to the clergy of the National Church of Iceland and discuss the need for the Church to contribute to social progress through humanitarian work. This led to the Church's founding of the Children's Home Committee with Rev. Guðmundur Einarsson of Mosfell as its chairman. Under his leadership, funds were raised by the Church through a series of campaigns, and the results exceeded all expectations. In 1930—the same year that Sesselja returned to Iceland—the Children's Home Committee decided to purchase an abandoned farm area in South Iceland called Hverakot for ISK 8,000 ($58 USD), and on the same day, leased it to Sesselja so that she could actualize her dream of creating a safe haven for children in need.

Building Commencement: The Beginning of Sólheimar

On her 28th birthday on July 5, 1930, Sesselja moved to the Hverakot land that she leased from the Children's Home Committee and founded her children's home there; thus began the operation of Sólheimar. The first five children

Sesselja was also a pioneer in organic plant cultivation—not only in Iceland but in the Nordic countries—and can be regarded as Iceland's first environmental activist.

She raised a large number of foster children and was a pioneer in pedagogy and care methods for children with developmental disabilities in Iceland.

arrived on that day, and soon afterward, another five arrived.

Sólheimar was originally established as a children's home, specifically for children with difficult family circumstances (e.g., following their parents' death or serious illness). The first child with developmental disabilities later arrived in 1931, when there were no facilities anywhere in Iceland to provide support for such children. There were, in fact, cases where these children were simply abandoned and kept in outbuildings.

When Sesselja leased the land from the Church, there were no habitable buildings on the estate. The residents initially lived in tents, but in the summer of that first year, Sesselja's brother Lúðvík was able to build wooden floors so that heating could be installed from the hot springs below for the structure above. During that autumn, building work commenced on a wooden house with an attic floor and a concrete basement. By November 4th, the building was roofed and weathertight, and the residents moved into the basement. Construction work continued throughout the winter to complete the interior of the house with the help of three young builders, including a skilled artisan German woodcarver named Reinholt. His work in an anthroposophical style lent a special character to the interior and the furnishings of the home.

When Sólheimar eventually became a self-owned organization on January 12, 1934, the Children's Home Committee gave the land of Hverakot to the village as its contribution to the incredible work that Sesselja was doing for the children and the community.

Sesselja made a point of saying that "Sólheimar was a home, not an institution, and that everyone there, whether they suffered from disabilities or not, shared the same conditions and daily life and work."

It was at Sólheimar that the principle of mixing persons with disabilities with others without

One of her fundamental beliefs was that children needed space to roam, run, and exercise. Previously, these kids were stigmatized and largely cooped up in buildings and institutions; the program was geared toward those kids. But other orphans were welcomed in as well.

Sesselja's bedroom for her 42 years at Sólheimar in Sólheimahús—now acting as a historical museum in the ecovillage, honoring the history and legacy of Sesselja and Sólheimar.

disabilities first emerged; it was not known abroad until about the 1970s.

Attic Room
From 1930 when Sólheimar was built and up until her death, Sesselja lived in the room on the attic floor of *Sólheimahús*, the first home built on the land of Hverakot. If a child—whether disabled or not—was ill, Sesselja would bring them into her own room and take care of them during the night. Here in the attic, staff and residents could come to Sesselja at any time of the day or night. Sesselja seemed to not need much sleep; she often stayed up late in the evening writing letters to her many correspondents in Iceland and abroad.

The desk from which she wrote hundreds and hundreds of letters—endlessly gathering support and volunteers.

Arts and Culture
Arts and culture played an important role in Sesselja's work at Sólheimar from the start. In 1931, the first play was produced, and that tradition has continued every year since. During his time at Sólheimar, Rudolf Noah, a German musician and teacher whom Sesselja later

Sólheimahús, the first home where Sesselja and the children lived.

Music is one of the main ways children at Sólheimar can explore their creativity.

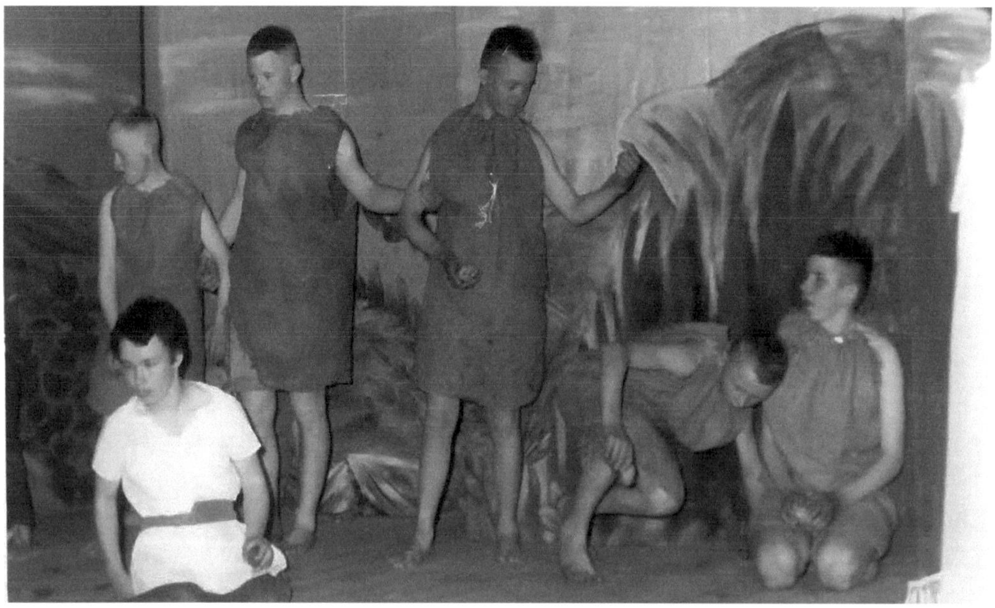

"The Big Play," which is still an annual event, has also played an important part in the creative culture at Sólheimar since the beginning.

married in 1949, took responsibility for the drama projects. He studied music and singing in Hamburg and pedagogy in Dornach and had great experience working with "problem" children in Germany and Switzerland. At Sólheimar, Rudolf played piano for the children in the dining room and taught them to sing and play musical instruments as well.

Under Noah's direction, drama activities were upgraded: he set up a puppet theatre, built a stage and sets, made costumes with the children, and rehearsed plays with them.

As with every aspect of life at Sólheimar, both children and adults with and without disabilities took part in the drama productions. And even though the children may not have understood everything that happened on the stage, history shows they were heavily influenced and educated by the plays.

In addition to the annual big play, music also played a vital role at Sólheimar from the outset. The children received music instruction from trained musicians long before it was introduced in Icelandic elementary schools, and various musical instruments were acquired from abroad or made on-site.

Vegetables Diet and Cuisine at Sólheimar

Sesselja integrated vegetables into the daily life of Sólheimar from the very beginning. At a time when most Icelanders lived on a diet of meat, she felt strongly about adding fresh vegetables. While the children's diet still included meat, fish, and dairy, the primarily plant-based diet was initially met with considerable criticism; official reports claimed that the children were not fed enough meat. Sesselja emphasized what are now called "organic" methods of horticulture, and from the foundation of Sólheimar, all its activities were consistent with what we now call "sustainable development." Sólheimar was thus, from the very first day, a sustainable community—perhaps the first in the modern/post-industrial revolution world.

Hard Times

In the early years at Sólheimar, many of the staff were foreigners. These individuals had been trained and worked in a range of fields, such as music, woodcarving, nursing, cookery, gardening, and childcare, and they brought new influences with them. They were idealists. A few of them got a salary for their work, but many did not. After the outbreak of World War II in 1939, foreign staff were no longer able to come to Sólheimar to work. For a time, the enterprise was sustained by Sesselja's friends and family. Her aged father and her sisters came to assist her; in 1944, Sesselja's brother Thórarinn moved to Sólheimar with his family and stayed for two years. He ran the farm while his wife, Ingibjorg, was a teacher.

Criticism and Scrutiny

The work at Sólheimar often encountered distrust. Child protection legislation was passed in 1932, and soon afterward, conflict arose between Sesselja and the authorities that continued for the following decades. The authorities were opposed to children with and without disabilities being housed together at Sólheimar, and the vegetable-heavy diet was also a contentious issue. For many years, all reports on the health of the children focused on the milk they

The morning circle has been practiced from the beginning. This picture is from 1931.

drank and whether they gained weight. That appears to have been the only index of progress that was regarded as valid, although the health of the children was unusually good.

Sesselja Under Attack
Sólheimar was under constant attack from the authorities, and on July 4, 1945, the Child Protection Board ruled that Sesselja should be stripped of the right to be the director of Sólheimar. This setback did not diminish Sesselja's conviction, however. She refused to leave and decided to appeal the case to the Icelandic Supreme Court. The Child Protection Board took offense at Sesselja's defiance, and the Minister of Education was urged to take action. Sesselja had friends who came to her aid: one of these was the Bishop of Iceland, who visited Sólheimar. He wrote a report in which he stood up for Sesselja: "The problems of the children's home," he concluded, "arose from lack of funding and shortage of staff." The Bishop praised her work and the groundbreaking project she had launched, as did Iceland's Director of Health.

The early 1940s were the most difficult period in the history of Sólheimar, yet Sesselja strove to ensure that the children's lives were not affected. These were challenging years for Sesselja, who faced many of Sólheimar's struggles alone. But her conviction never wavered, and she toiled tirelessly day and night to continue the important work happening at Sólheimar.

Saved at the Eleventh Hour
In 1946, the Minister of Education decided it was time to act. Emergency legislation was introduced on the 12th of September, providing authority for the closure of the children's home at Sólheimar. But as luck would have it, the government fell in October, and a general election ensued. Hence, the emergency legislation was never passed by parliament, and it expired. It has been said that it was "God's hand protecting Sesselja and her conviction for Sólheimar." Later, in 1948, the Icelandic Supreme Court picked up the case again and, this time, judged in her favor. On the night after the trial, Sesselja came back to her attic room and wrote only two words in her diary: "case won."

The "mixing" of capabilities proved to be a major growth experience for all participants of all capacities. There are no children at Sólheimar today. They say that Iceland virtually no longer has any orphans; whether they're developmentally challenged or not, they are adopted or in foster care of some sort.

Talking with peers, kibitzing, and knowing each other for decades; these behaviors transform friendships into deep, meaningful relationships and, ultimately, to family.

Most new residents in Sólheimar today are young adults, usually in their 20s, who want to move out of their parents' house. At Sólheimar, they gain considerable independence through employment, purpose, and community.

Sesselja's work continued. From that time onward, Sólheimar was a home exclusively for children with disabilities, apart from Sesselja's own foster children.

"I'll Find a Way."

Sesselja's clear organizational and leadership talents made her a perfect grassroots organizer. People simply believed in her and her vision.

Despite the lack of funding for Sólheimar, she firmly believed that the community would endure. And since no major accidents or injuries occurred—despite the primitive conditions in the early years—funding eventually did come through. The government saw the numerous benefits of Sesselja's methods, as did a particularly motivated and talented covey of teachers and volunteers. Her approach to growing vegetables, spending days outside, and cultivating a community became highly appreciated by parents, volunteers, and staff, and, most importantly, by the residents of Sólheimar. The beauty and value there became and still are palpable.

All of that being said, there is a regulatory role for the government, but it should exist to provide support and not be heavy-handed. Governments tend to institutionalize this kind of housing/care; instead of valuing creativity and entrepreneurialism, complicated legal barriers force them to return to the rule books. Some regulations are critical, but they need to be flexible and evolve to benefit the people and cultures being governed. These regulations should not create obstacles but should provide efficient, unwavering support for affected people when they need it.

Who is the affected community? What is it about? Why? It is a long and belabored process required to clearly and deliberately manifest the ideal of "One Life, Live It!"

CHAPTER 2

Given what we are still struggling with and can't seem to get out of (people with autism cast adrift and lonely), only the visionary's will can get us out of this.

Sólheimar Today: The Community

Sesselja had a vision. She intended to ensure that all children—especially those with disabilities—not be cast adrift. When we recognize that the way we currently do things is flawed, we can start to envision a better way forward: the only realist is the visionary. Sesselja realized that manifesting a clear vision is the only way to create meaningful change, and her vision was clear. All children—all people—deserve a community that is not only conducive to their well-being but one in which all the necessary components for complete and happy lives exist: purpose, friends, art, and love. Sesselja's intention from Sólheimar's conception was to be inclusive—that is, to design the entire environment for handicapped children while also integrating neurotypical children through "reverse integration." But the government gave her flack for that. In fact, at that time, the requirement was to fence in play yards to provide separation, which was antithetical to her beliefs. But the law didn't say how high the fence had to be, so Sesselja simply built it a few inches high so that her people could just step over it. It's been said that Sesselja took inspiration from the rocks that surrounded her in all directions, from the strength of nature itself. The fire in her heart was as impenetrable as the rocky landscape that surrounded her.

DOI: 10.4324/9781003642336-3

The daily morning circle: an important place for village news, ritual, and routine.

On Language
I have chosen to use both person-first and identity-first language to reflect the feedback of various self-advocates and their families that I have encountered. Additionally, it must be recognized that other countries may use different terms than what is common in the U.S. I ask that readers approach this book with intention and not be distracted by word choice. It must be recognized that many of these interviews are with older people with autism (80+) who use the language of their time.

Daily Life at Sólheimar
Sesselja's vision necessitated structure; there is a predictable flow to the days at Sólheimar. Life for the residents (the "home people," as they often refer to themselves) is quite routine and predictable. The workday is seven hours, and it has a gentle rhythm to it.

Morning
In the morning, residents have breakfast at home, with their housemates, or alone. They then head over to the daily morning circle: an important source of village news, ritual, and routine. With information and co-management, the morning circle is a critical source of formalized—but not regimented—interaction that leads to everyone being informed about opportunities. Not everyone follows every routine but does so enough to share with others at their own pace and keep community members in the loop. "Today we will have visitors from the music department of the university. If you are thinking about picking up a new instrument, they are meeting at the main theatre at 1:00 pm." If that comes up three times in one week, there will be twice as much participation as if it only came up once and ten times more participation than if it came out in an email.

A Ritual for the Kind

"An Essay on the Morning Meeting" by Aurora K., former volunteer at Sólheimar, from January 5, 2020

The sun has not risen. The sky is darkened by the hushed voices of the people who still lie in bed. Sometimes, one can see stars or the slight glimpse of an orange sun beyond the valley. The air is brisk against warm, flushed cheeks. Sheep graze on the dewed grass before winter begins. And when the winter season breathes its way into the land, snow falls on the lashes of those who walk quickly towards the warmth of the building.

Each morning, the bells from the church that watches over Sólheimar will sound at a constant speed, nine times for the hour. Ten minutes before, the sleepy eyes of the home people walk into the doors of the grey building, smiling to keep themselves a bit more awake. They take off their shoes in the entryway. Sometimes coats. They laugh. They talk. They are aware of the love that surrounds them. It's palpable; long-term relationships lead to total acceptance, and that leads to relaxing and being yourself. The black cat, Gary, a pet owned by one of the home people, walks into the building as if no one is watching.

Past the entryway is a large room with a gym, a wood floor, and a small, theatre-like stage behind. There are basketball hoops on the pink-clouded walls. The lighting is dim.

Every minute until nine, more people come into the room with high ceilings. They begin to hold hands with one another, eventually forming a circle where each person faces another. There are about fifteen to twenty people each morning. Not everyone from the village comes. The volunteers are rare to see. But usually, the same faces show up—the same smiles, the same laughter. There are regulars. There are more when the weather is nice and less when the weather is poor. More when it is at the end of the week than the beginning. Sometimes, there are new faces—visitors to Sólheimar, guests who observe the meeting. They are greeted with kindness and a hand to hold.

The bells chime nine times. Last-minute arrivals join in the circle. When the bells cease, those in the circle raise up their embraced clasps and state, "Góðan daginn," Good morning. They let go of the others' hands for a moment's time.

The meeting begins. Some will say things about the weather. Some will talk about events they are excited about. Some will say something about what is on their minds. The lunch for the day will be announced. The staff will share important activities going on in Sólheimar. A birthday could be shared. Visitors are introduced. Achievements will be acknowledged and applauded. It is like popcorn bouncing off the echoed room. The cat will run through the circle, distracting those from the conversation at hand. But the exchange only lasts for five minutes. Sometimes less, sometimes more.

After all that needed to be said has been said, hands will again be joined. In unison, a song will be sung. A choir of voices will fill the bellies of the folk who smile at each person through a soft ripple of sounds through the village. When the morning meeting is over, an English version will be repeated in a small group. The rest leave the scene: on with their workshops, their own routines, perhaps breakfast. The day begins.

Implications of the Meeting

The morning meeting exists as almost a ritual that blends the ideals of cohousing with those of a family gathering. It is like a business meeting, but where everyone supports one another through holding hands and singing. It is a very strange thing for one at first, but as time goes on, it seems almost a normal way of life. It is a way to make people feel more comfortable with the passing of time, to make the home people feel at peace when life gets too busy. It brings together the aspects of society, politics, economics, and happiness all in one building in one morning. It makes the home people feel as included as they feel in Sólheimar. This is the only meeting per day when the home people feel they get their say in a peaceful state. Sólheimar still has a long way to go to flatten its management and to be even more inclusive, but the circle accomplishes some of this.

—Aurora K

There's a morning coffee break, and each workshop has a cozy area to gather and spend breaks together twice per day. This formality, basically "teatime," facilitates more efficient work, and it definitely facilitates community.

Noon

After the morning circle, the day has begun: residents are off to various workshops, classes, or events. See Chapter 4 for all the activities that are offered.

At noon, residents head over to the Græna Kannan Café for common lunch, where they connect with friends to talk about their day, plan social events for the week, talk about choir practice, and catch up. They are served lunch with homemade breads and a self-serve salad bar. Lunch usually includes a mix of Icelandic cuisine and vegetarian dishes. The meat dishes might be lamb, beef, chicken, or seafood, but vegetarian options are always available: a variety of steamed vegetables, mashed or roasted potatoes, carrots, cauliflower, broccoli, onion, lentils, and corn. Sometimes desserts are offered, and there is always coffee. There is an emphasis placed on consistently serving healthy, nutrient-dense meals.

It is hard to imagine autistic folks being comfortable with 40 or 50 people in one place, but every person is more or less familiar to them. They have been "introduced" to each other over the years. They work interdependently with each other, they give to each other, and they receive from one another. They become emotionally interdependent. I've observed that they are extremely comfortable—compared to other autistic people interacting with the general public—because they are thriving, they feel safe, and they are at ease with their relationships here. They have had a lot of practice.

"What are you doing after work today? Let's go for a walk or something." Breaking bread not only provides physical sustenance, but important social sustenance as well.

Measuring the happiness metrics here is easy: words spoken per half-hour, smiles per half-hour, eye contact instances per half-hour, touches per half-hour–these are all important metrics. The happiness movement has made an art and science of measuring happiness, including hours of conversing per day, hours in the common areas per day, and, most importantly, gross (total) people hours in the common house per week. There are important aspects of synergy contributing to an aggregate sum. I want to be in the common house because Jim is in the common house, and Jane wants to be in the common house because I'm in the common house; these communal human tendencies really are foundational insights for this book.

Some people sit at the same table day after day, but most do not. They sit wherever they feel like, with whoever they want. These interactions evolve over the years as people become more and more socially comfortable. Sometimes, the interactions are based on who they "need" to talk to that day because they have questions or opinions that they want to express. Sometimes, they want to have a casual, brief interaction, or they want to just listen or follow up on that deeply philosophical conversation that they had yesterday with their friends.

Their lives have shifted 180 degrees from what they were before—they're more socially engaged than in previous self-isolation. Everyone should have this opportunity to develop.

When You Know It's the Right Thing To Do, Stay Determined and Persevere

Though now praised for their healthy diet, back in the formative days of Sólheimar, it was difficult to serve predominantly plant-based meals. Diet is an evolving topic at Sólheimar, just like in the larger world. Diet brings the home people something to talk about; it is one big common denominator. Now, we know better than they did when plant-based diets were ridiculed, but there always seems to be at least one bureaucratic barrier in the way of progress. Maybe it's a matter of less or more thoughtful bureaucracy, more support, and better responsiveness.

Afternoon

Lunch lasts from noon to one, after which residents return to the workshops and greenhouses or go to activities like dancing and practicing for the play—the highlights of keeping people connected. And there is always an afternoon coffee/tea break.

The café is open until 5pm most days and is often open on weekends. It offers coffee, cakes, tea, sandwiches, pies, and cookies, as well as vegan, gluten-free, sugar-free, and dairy-free options. Visitors pay for lunch, but it is included in the residents' rent.

In the evening, the residents go on walks, cook dinner, and relax with their roommates, clean up, hang out with their neighbors, or just enjoy their alone time. Dinner is at the individual residences, and common dinner is cooked and shared at the shared houses (of which two are co-living housing types—see Chapter 3).

Monday through Friday provide plenty of opportunities to come together. People strive to become better artisans and better neighbors freely and independently. Alone time is pursued as needed. Most people, however, choose to be around one another—enjoying each other's company, conversation, and frequent music-making.

A resident doesn't have to work at Sólheimar, but they are introduced to many possibilities that might be intriguing or fancy their curiosities, and most end up getting involved. People work because they want to; they want to have a purpose, something to do, and something to continuously strive for. There's almost a guild culture: "As long as we're doing this, we might as well learn how to do it well. I might as well be an artisan." They each want recognition as someone who knows how to do something, who contributes, and who will always have something they can proudly talk about. And it is nice to have money to buy discretionary things.

I've been to a lot of conferences and lived in cohousing for the last 34 years, and I've never seen anyone as capable of efficiently bussing their own dishes as the residents of Sólheimar.

The All-Important Third Place

As a source of sustenance, Græna Kannan café provides a third place for the community. It's not home; it's not work; it's where the village comes to meet up with each other throughout the day to sit and chat with neighbors and friends, both old and new.

The wooden tables, the pendant lights, and the sloped ceilings all create an inviting place to have lunch and host other events. Lots of light, lots of warmth, and plenty of comfortable furniture—this place is a metaphorical greenhouse where many seeds are planted. "Hey, might we take Saturday's visitors on a hike?" is an example of what one might propose to a friend at the café.

Community and purpose are arguably the greatest drivers and sources of increasing and facilitating emotional well-being. This man runs a one-man post office for the community.

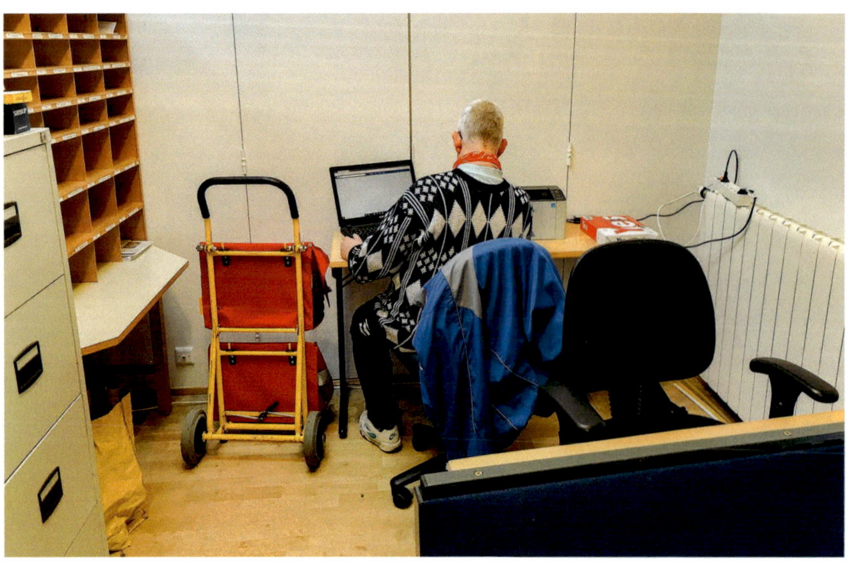

Mixing Up the Routine

Life could become too routine if it weren't for the flexibility of switching jobs when someone wants to. One might go from weaving and knitting to mechanical maintenance or gardening outdoors to woodworking in the shop. Some prefer perfecting their craft, whatever that might be. Others, especially those living with associated ADHD, tend towards variety, but not always. The only rule is to let folks follow their curiosities—curiosity will motivate you like nothing else. In Einstein's biography, he said that he didn't love formal education because it didn't adequately allow him to follow his curiosities. After college, he followed his curiosities and came up with a few good ideas. See Chapter 4.

Blossoming into Your Best Self

Sólheimar thrives on the very idea of community. Most arrive quite reserved, mostly because they haven't been active in thriving social settings. At Sólheimar, people are engaged in a variety of activities: social, practical, domestic, artistic, cultural, physical, and so on. These acts require serious communication, engagement, language, logistics, and more, so the residents don't usually remain timid or withdrawn for long. But there are still plenty of opportunities to be alone in their rooms if and when they want to.

Data shows that about 60% of the neuro-typical population is extroverted, and about 40% is introverted. That is the case at Sólheimar as well, though people don't come to express their more natural social inclinations until they've spent a year or two there. These inclinations come to you when you are fortunate enough to live in a thriving community.

Margarita, a former Project Manager, told us, "What is amazing is that those diagnosed with autism are supposedly 'bad' in social situations." But perhaps this is

Arnar moved in at 34 years old. Previously, he never had a job and had only one to two hours of peer interaction per week. He was shy and rarely smiled when he first moved into Sólheimar, but then he started getting 25–30 hours of peer interaction per week (or as much as he desired).

When I asked him, "Arnar, why are you always smiling?" he said, "I have something to do every day, people depend on me, I depend on them, we're a team, now I have purpose. I'm on the maintenance team. I scrape wood with my scraper, someone else sands the woodwork (mostly around the windows), someone else masks off the windows, someone else primes them, and someone else paints them. I have tools, I have equipment, I have skills. I'm accepted and appreciated, and I respect myself. I have purpose, and therefore, I'm a lot happier."

The postman takes a break with his friends and neighbors. This resident delivers the mail and takes it seriously. He is also an organizer of the local used bookstore at Sólheimar. He has clearly thrived in his role as a neighbor and Sólheimar's sole postman.

only the case when they're in a new environment, exasperated or uneasy like introverts in awkward new relationships. With seasoned relationships, these interactions not only become easier but become a vital component of life. When someone is in isolation—essentially in solitary confinement—their social needs and personal potential cannot be fulfilled. But I never once saw this condition amongst seasoned relationships in Sólheimar, apart from when someone first moved in. Once one becomes familiar with others, there is joking and teasing more like that of siblings than just neighbors in a functional neighborhood.

Reynir Pétur, left, moved in at 5 years old, and Ólafur, right, moved in when he was 3. They are now both in their eighties. Those at Sólheimar have had statistically much greater success than their peers born elsewhere without the same kind of environment, who have not fared nearly as well. Children no longer move into Sólheimar.

You constantly hear parents say to their young adult children, "Johnny, you just need to get out to make new friends." Malarkey. What Johnny needs is a band of old friends. That's where Johnny lets down his hair, relaxes, relates, jokes, and feels accepted and included. This only happens in a community with longevity. You can't buy longevity, but you can build it by involving everyone in evolution. Involve as many people as possible in the origin story and the evolution story.

New residents have their own challenges, of course. Most are more reserved and shyer than those who have been here for several years.

When folks with midrange autism first move into Sólheimar, they usually have some difficulty with peer interaction. Later in his residency, this young man relaxed. Within a month, folks usually begin to come out of their shell, lose some reservations, and become part of the community.

Reynir, left, and Gunnar, right, have lived here for over 70 and 60 years, respectively. They have had full and amazing lives. Google Reynir and you will see some of his exploits. Sólheimar handed him a full life with the security that he needed and the support provided to him by people who knew and cared about him. This made him feel safe enough to circumnavigate Iceland by foot (1,500 miles).

Impressions of Sólheimar from an American Volunteer

"Ruminating on Sólheimar" by Aurora Kuczek

One part of the village that makes Sólheimar special is the setting. Iceland has a unique geography. With no trees and a lot of rocks dusting the horizon, it looks like another planet. In addition to that, the stark cold makes it so much easier for people to gather indoors and talk to one another. But apart from this, I found that the Icelanders spoke with a different tenor compared to other cultures. They were caring, selfless, and genuine people—not just the people of Sólheimar but the whole country itself. It was as if they were raised on goodness; they were made to help other people.

Everyone in Sólheimar has many friends. They are intuitive friends with wide arms and big smiles. You may not get along with each and every person you meet, but you have to coexist. That is one very important lesson I learned from Sólheimar: the concept of coexisting.

Sólheimar forms relationships, maintains relationships, and nourishes them. People come because they realize there is more to life than living for themselves. There can be unsubsidized happiness knowing that one is helping another person—**knowing that one is fueling someone else's energy as well as their own.** I believe that real purpose is achieved by working in a community like Sólheimar and supporting those who cannot live life productively on their own without a cohousing society.

The author with Gunnar, a resident at Sólheimar.

Functioning Neighborhoods Help

When I was a kid, I lived in a small town in Sierra County, California. Across the street from me lived a young man, Sam, with midrange intellectual challenges. Everyone in town played a role in helping him succeed. Everything from, "Sam, don't stand in the street," to remind him that "It's going to be dark soon, Sam. Can I walk you home?" Everyone, including myself, even in my teens, felt like it would be a failure for all of us if something happened to Sam.

Never once did anyone call the police on Sam for his aberrant behavior—we simply sat down and talked to him. We could do that because people talked to each other in that town. It wasn't just about helping Sam; his Italian mom needed and appreciated the help, as did his older sister. This kind of cooperation benefits not just the family but society at large: it keeps Sam from bothering everyone (especially tourists), keeping costs down, kept police calls to a minimum, kept someone from being criminalized for their condition (prisons are filled with people with mental disabilities), and kept Sam from hurting himself. The support of his neighbors kept Sam from being berated by bullies so that his self-esteem would not hit rock bottom. Sam still thrives today: watering people's lawns in the summer, shoveling snow in the winter, and more.

People with Autism and Down Syndrome Thrive in Community

This is a complex issue. Although I am not a mental health professional, I've learned from them that there is no real consensus. This brief overview incorporates personal, anecdotal experience and the knowledge that Sólheimar's 94 years of existence have provided.

This book only covers two neurological conditions which Sólheimar accommodates best: medium-range autism and Down syndrome. Please keep in mind that everyone's experience is unique, and each will need care that is specific to them and their needs.

As an architect of such a vast array of housing types, I've had to learn what works empirically and which environments suit different users: neurologically diverse housing, all-Hmong housing, homeless housing, worker housing in Africa, a school for children with cerebral palsy that used horseback riding as a major pedagogical and physiotherapy tool, and more. This book is a study and practice of appropriate placemaking.

Autism Spectrum Disorder

Autism Spectrum Disorder (ASD) is a neurological and developmental disorder that affects how people interact with others, communicate, learn, and behave. It is sometimes accompanied by other neurodivergence, such as ADHD.

ASD is a neurodevelopmental disorder normally characterized by deficits and challenges in social skills. It is also characterized by repetitive and/or restrictive patterns of behaviors and interests. Symptoms vary from

Day after day, people get together. This is how you help individuals: make a village and a functioning society.

People have the choice to be alone or together, but as they spend more time in the village, they grow together and want to spend more time together.

being non-verbal to being barely noticeable. Symptoms can manifest quite differently in each person; behavior varies considerably and is dependent on how well supported the person has been as well as by their particular genetics. The causes of ASD are not widely understood but appear to be mostly genetic and inherited. Since they are so misunderstood (thousands of genes are involved), and because the clear onset and varied manifestations occur at different times in life, there has been a lot of speculation about environmental causes such as benzenes and vaccines. Environmental conditions may play a role in the development of ASD, but that will remain speculation until the very complicated genetic questions are better objectified.

Autism Symptoms Can Include:

- Difficulty communicating and engaging in social interactions
- Avoidance of eye contact
- Hypersensitivity: emotional and tactual
- Repetition of words and motions
- Difficulty engaging in education and employment
- Misreading/trouble reading body language
- Learning disabilities

People ages 13–18 sometimes need much more support; they may even need paid staff.

A non-thriving autistic person in distress can develop co-morbidities such as anxiety, OCD, eating disorders, ADHD and other illnesses that can lead to self-harm and other consequences.

Autism Best Practices by Neighbors:

- Take them seriously
- Never be condescending
- Be careful what you say; be extra sensitive
- Accept them: if they feel accepted, they will, therefore, be much more relaxed in your presence

Greta Thunberg is probably one of the most famous people on the spectrum today. Having autism allows her to analyze difficult-to-process information about climate change, speak truth to power, and be incredibly direct when communicating. She can't imagine why we are not taking man-made climate change more seriously, and she refers to this as her superpower: "I have [autism] and that means I'm sometimes a bit different from the norm," she tweeted. "And—given the right circumstances—being different is a superpower." That is perhaps the direct single-mindedness we need right now. Another champion for the autism awareness movement is Temple Grandin. She has reached her potential through exceptional educational opportunities and a relentless drive for self-improvement. And while her global network of supporters is invaluable, it's the immediate, local community that has had the most direct impact on her success. Alongside Grandin and Thunberg, there are many other notable individuals on the spectrum, such as Dan Aykroyd, Anthony Hopkins, Susan Boyle, and Bill Gates.

History is chock full of people now believed to have had autism: Hans Christian Andersen, Charles Darwin, Albert Einstein, Steve Jobs, James Joyce, Stanley Kubrick, Bobby Fischer, and millions more. However, this book isn't about those exceptional cases. It's about the everyday quality of life.

The skills necessary to communicate effectively with a person with ASD are being kind, being a good listener, being empathetic, and being able to articulate your needs as calmly and as deliberately as possible. Sólheimar uses a Support Intensity Scale (which describes a spectrum of capabilities and support needs) from 1–18 to determine who qualifies to live there. Those between 1–6 are considered capable enough to live successfully and independently elsewhere. People with needs in the range of 7–12 on the spectrum are considered perfect candidates for reaching their potential by living in a supportive, semi-independent setting like Sólheimar. People with needs in the range of 13–18 need much more hands-on care than they can provide at Sólheimar.

There are certain universal practices, such as non-violent communication, that are necessary for living in a mutually supportive community. Raised voices and yelling are rare in a functioning community, except in an emergency. Extreme impatience doesn't work well; exasperation and frustration are mitigated well when folks choose to work on and prioritize relationships.

It is proven that folks with midrange autism thrive in the community; that has been made abundantly clear by the success of Sólheimar. When people between 7–12 on the ASD spectrum are employed, given purpose, accepted as friends, figure out who they are and how they can fit in, and are given something to talk about, they thrive. This range is usually considered dysfunctional unless one lives in a care or community setting—which Sólheimar has successfully proved. This midrange population is capable of accomplishing many of their necessary daily functions themselves. Tasks and activities

Friends being friends is the beginning and end of figuring out this whole life deal together.

such as fixing meals, dressing, riding a bike, taking a shower, doing laundry, ambulating (walking around without falling), making art and going to classes, working certain jobs, and other Activities of Daily Living (ADLs) are achieved in these environments.

I once had an employee, "Susan," who had to move back home because her older autistic brother would act out about once a month in public and consequently suffer beatings or social abuse. When her mother became terminally ill, Susan, who was 23 years old, had to move back home to keep her brother out of trouble. Not considering social boundaries, not understanding the difference between pleasantries and crossing the line, or not knowing the difference between "Excuse me, I need to get by" and "GET OUT OF MY WAY" can result in harmful consequences. Thank goodness that he had a sister willing to help him; not everyone does. I don't think that these problems would have persisted if Susan's brother lived in a supportive community. There is a steady dose of accountability and an abundance of love. These treatments seriously mitigate bad behavior. A young, talented professional who wants to blossom as an architect may not be able to do so because of insufficient caregiving scenarios like this one.

It's harder—or impossible—to learn these boundaries in a home, unlike in an interactive social setting. Like Sólheimar, some societies are accepting; the scale of Sólheimar itself makes it infinitely easier than living in a big, anonymous city.

In my conversation with one of the Social Educators, Dagný, she told me that many people with autism feel safer in a smaller place:

> *It's a place where they can feel safe, where we can take care of people and help them be independent. They're part of a society here, part of a community. They can walk wherever they want without the traffic, stress, and everything that comes with being in a city.*

How Do They Determine Who Gets to Live in Sólheimar?

Sólheimar does have a waiting list, and they decide who to admit based on "who can we do the best for." Social services within different municipalities of Iceland have a waiting list of about three to five people each, and the social workers at Sólheimar choose who to extend invitations to from that list. The prospective residents then visit to see if they want to live there—ultimately, it's a choice. Sólheimar accepts residents from 64 municipalities across the eight regions of Iceland. There are dozens of people at any given time who want to live there, but they do the social math carefully and know how to keep it just the right size. See Chapter 3.

People occasionally move into Sólheimar who are not exactly midrange. Sometimes, these folks move out because they either need more care or they want more independence in their own space, but some of them do end up staying at Sólheimar.

Down Syndrome
Unlike with autism, there is consensus on what causes Down syndrome: an extra 21st chromosome of the 46 chromosomes in the body. The small package of 200–300 genes inside the extra chromosome wreaks

"Personhood"

"My autism dances with my personhood . . . and my personhood must also dance with my autism—yet not whilst separable, nor are they interchangeable with each other."
Donna Williams

After enduring a childhood marked by unimaginable abuse, Donna Williams, known affectionately as 'Polly,' was left with deep emotional and physical scars, including severe PTSD and a range of other health struggles. Her early years were filled with isolation, where she began sleeping on the streets, but at the age of 13, Polly's life began to take a turn for the better when she found her way to an informal foster home.

Though the trauma of her past never fully left her, Polly discovered a sense of community among a close-knit group of friends. Polly's path would eventually cross with Chris, a man who would change her life in profound ways. Their love brought stability, understanding, and joy, and Chris remained by her side until her passing in 2017.

Through these relationships, Polly not only began a lifelong journey of emotional healing but also began to receive the medical care she had long needed, giving her a chance to take control of her health and begin the process of rebuilding her life.

Romantic relations happen. They are sometimes part of "One Life, Live It!" There are those who believe that sex education should always be part of the curriculum, stressing, "when comfortable, when appropriate," which can be challenging for both people with and without autism.

These pivotal relationships were the people who, despite the darkness of her past, helped guide her toward a future filled with love, hope, and the possibility of peace. 'Polly,' under the name of Donna Williams, became an author, singer-songwriter, screenwriter, and sculptor. Her work has inspired millions, including this author; see Appendix A for more information. She said:

> *I found a diamond of a person and he shone so bright I asked him to marry me. We are often surprised when people mention an autistic marriage. How can two people, strong enough in their own worlds to be called autistic, find someone with whom to have a meeting of hearts and minds for life? Yet we all have autistic moments and marriage sustains these. We can have an autistic life while both partners are comfortable and at home in that autistic reality; autism may be an asset more than an obstacle.*
>
> *A marriage is a ceremony recognizing the joining of hearts and minds between a couple choosing one another as their life partners. Autistic hearts and minds are just as capable of finding that connection and making that commitment as any human being.*

There are communities with a wide variety of diagnoses; some symptoms can be discerned theoretically, but there is mostly empirical evidence. Alcoholism, for example, is now a diagnosis—but alcoholics and other addicts do not always thrive in high-functioning community settings. That said, there is no one to say that individuals can't try to live where they choose to live other than for the administrators who often have havoc. The extra chromosome looks like the architectural letter "W."

Folks with Down syndrome have proven to thrive in the community and, conversely, suffer in excess isolation. Quincy Jones (1993–2024), the renowned global spokesperson for the Global Down Syndrome Foundation, famously said, "These children aren't broken, they just need a leg up, the chance to reach their potential." To allow neurotypical people to succeed in their relationships with community members or neighbors with autism or Down syndrome, please refer to the best practices section in the box below.

Down Syndrome Symptoms Can Include:

- Extreme sociability and positivity (most folks with Down syndrome thrive in the community)
- Mostly appropriate social behavior, though frustration is common due to difficulties with language

Down Syndrome Best Practices by Neighbors:

- Slow down your speech if they get frustrated (they will understand much more of what you say than what they themselves can articulate)
- If aberrant behavior is not unsafe, try ignoring it or giving no feedback
- Be patient, empathetic, and compassionate

to make the hard decisions for others. There are those who feel like no segregation should happen. This book, however, is designed to set individuals up with optimal, found families—there are no shoulds or should-nots beyond that.

The work yet to be done is to understand how to get people with these diagnoses into appropriate communities—and much of that work has begun worldwide. No one should be left out, including those with Dementia, Alzheimer's, Depression, Cerebral Palsy, etc.

I'm not saying that community is the remedy for every diagnosis, but I am saying that it is a better alternative solution for some diagnosed people. And it can be the difference between life and death for many. Too many diagnosed people are neglected, and many commit suicide or waste away.

As I/DD activist Desiree Kameka Galloway, director of Autism Housing Networks, said,

> *In the USA, many bureaucrats, and some disability rights activists (often with just a physical disability) believe that any form of clustering people with disabilities or congregate living is institutional and thus they advocate that people with disabilities should not be housed close together. I and many others must push back on this constantly . . . we have found that self-advocates sharing that it is their preference to live in an intentional community is very helpful.*

It is also noted by activist Kameka Galloway that, "Personally, I think forced integration is just as dehumanizing as forced segregation, and people should have the right to 'integrate' as much as they please."

No level of dogma or righteousness is helpful. What is helpful is to observe, gain experience, collect data, and encourage a new path forward. After designing 55 cohousing communities for 55 different populations and observing hundreds of others, I began to understand what works best. This process took years and years. Some said that I took the Jane Goodall approach by studying and discerning who people are and who they want to be. This is the humanistic approach—not just a theoretical one, but an anthropological one. This book recognizes the potential for filling the gaps in our understanding of how cohousing can support people with disabilities.

CHAPTER 3

The job is to make a place where sharing beautiful moments together is easy and normal—not an exception. A choice and not a chore.

The Architecture of Sólheimar

Proximity is the secret ingredient to a village, and proximity and community are the secret ingredients to sustainability. Walking to get a croissant and coffee in the morning, walking to work, walking home for lunch, walking to buy bread, walking back to work, walking to various offices during the day, walking to the dentist, walking to the post office, walking back home at night, walking to the garden, picking up dinner supplies, stopping along the way to see a sick friend, running into a couple of acquaintances, catching up, making plans, and chatting: that's sustainability. That's a village. There are countless good reasons for a society to operate this way: the health of children (playmates next door, in close proximity); the health of seniors (not having to drive to see their friends and family); and the health of everyone in between. Additionally, infrastructure, water, sewer, gas, roads, retaining walls, etc., are less costly in a village. Pollution, albedo (reflected radiation affecting ambient temperature), waste, costs, physical threats (autos), and emotional threats (loneliness) are a lot higher in an estranged, auto-dominated environment.

DOI: 10.4324/9781003642336-4

The Ancient Chinese village concept, where the architecture embraces the topography, the community, and, in this case, the farm as well. By clustering the houses close to one another, more space is left for habitat, watershed, and nature. In an urban setting, it might embrace high-rises to the right and merchants to the left.

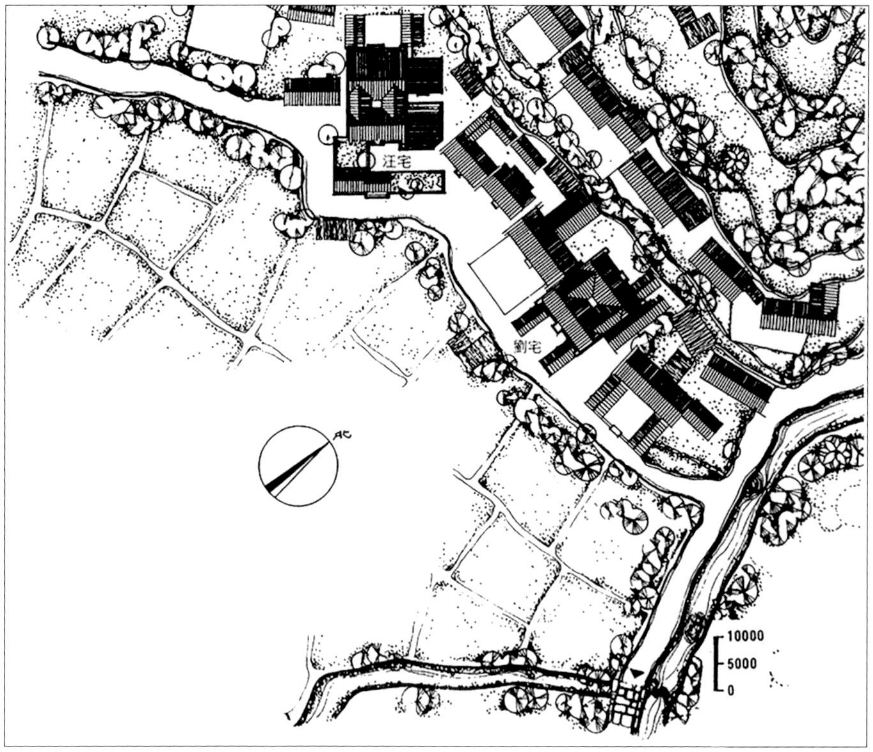

Medieval planning also works well. Mimic where and how people once walked or where and how the cows once walked. The settlement follows organically and makes it easy to do life's activities on foot.

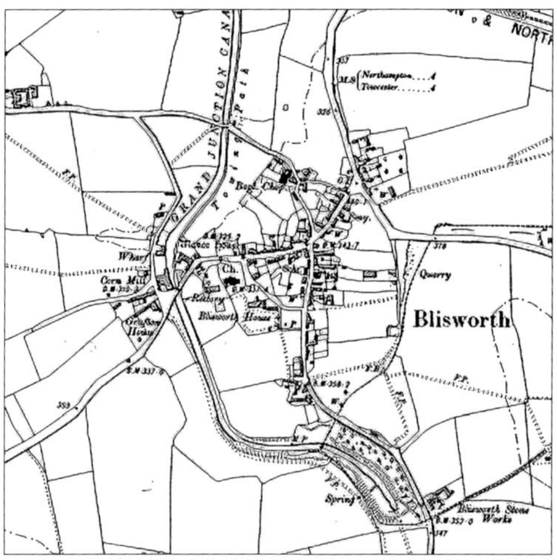

Home, church, work, school, pubs, restaurants, town administration buildings—everything is within easy walking distance. The community gathers at the outdoor plaza to sit, socialize, and commune; it's all right there.

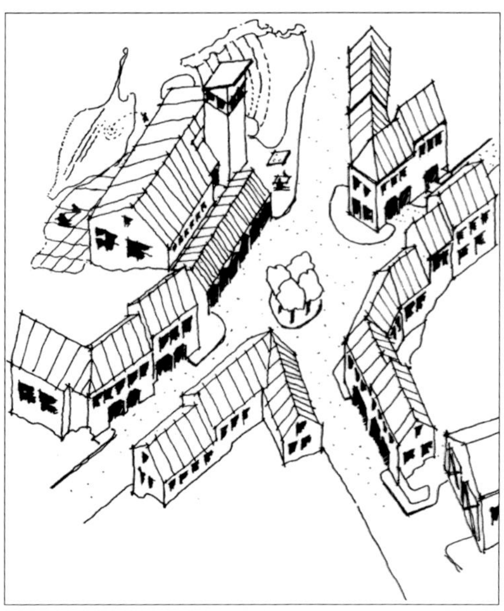

There are many discussions among architects about how to make the physical environments for autistic folks feel safe: mitigate trip hazards, remove sharp corners, get the acoustics right, get the lighting right, and so on. While these tactics work for everyone, they are critical for people with autism.

But, the huge missing elements for neurodivergent people are the social and emotional aspects: the places where people can sit and play the guitar and strike up a conversation with others that they know and care about. An environment where you walk out of your home and are forced into an uncomfortable social setting, where you lack control of your own emotional wellbeing, and your personal room is your only safe space—this is not a happy place. Solitary confinement is the most inhumane way to live, even when it's self-imposed.

A back door facilitates privacy, and a front porch facilitates connection—"If you sit here, it's at my invitation"—that's a privilege every person deserves but is not found in an institution, a shared house, or living at home with parents. The opportunity to control your environment allows for privacy (your room or back deck), semi-privacy (a front porch or dining table), or community (where talking, sitting around a fire, and eating and singing together are just natural extensions of your life).

"One Life, Live It!" encourages the creation of an environment where we can each live our best lives. This chapter is all about the physical community: how to make it so it is not only enduring and easy to maintain but also creates a sense of belonging, safety, connection, and happiness for everyone within.

A village has texture, varied colors, interest, detailed nuance, and very few missing teeth. It has places along the way to sit, to just be, and to commune. A village feels like a village.

Maintaining asphalt and gravel roads is unending, time-consuming, and expensive. Car-free, walkable villages are where people connect. It's an old-world pattern of human habitation that's reemerging because it still works best.

Village settings emphasize a continuation of place-making. They do not turn their back on history and are human-scale, compact, and intimate.

There is a special methodology for determining the success of a program. See the book Cohousing Communities: Designing for High-Functioning Neighborhoods.

Programming: Knowing Who We Are and Who We Want to Be

Architectural programming is the process that produces the set of criteria dictating the design and guides the eventual creation, formation, and evaluation of a project. The programming phase is really where the project is built—*not brick by brick, but decision by decision*—and where common vocabulary is established. Preferences and requirements are determined and built into the overall picture before time is invested in design. Programming is where the future inhabitants truly come to understand *who they are, who they aspire to be, and how their future neighborhood can support their goals, visions, and aspirations.*

In the beginning, before you draw a line, you must have predetermined goals and outcomes. It is about more than simulating other places; it is impossible to analyze preexisting programs in a timely fashion or adopt them to successfully direct your own designs. It is much better to understand what you want to accomplish by partnering with a competent programmer and creating specific criteria for your program and physical environment together—that's how you make your design fit like a glove. Spending time visiting other programs is an inefficient way to reach your goals—it can take months and even years. I have designed large projects where clients previously spent vast amounts of time analyzing similar case studies for inspiration and ended up creating confusing and irrelevant criteria that did not work for their project. At best, they reassessed and reestablished the criteria; at worst, they built a "replica" of other projects that was not appropriate for them and obviously neglected their goals.

A key purpose of programming is to reduce the need for later backtracking and redesign. Redesigning, especially after construction, costs a project thousands of people hours and thousands—if not millions—of dollars. A thorough programming process is essential for maintaining an orderly and cost-effective creation process later in the project. We find that many of the design problems people encounter in their projects (some rooms are too big, others too small, and many other challenges) can be avoided with a thorough programming process.

The few days of facilitated discussion change the trajectory of a project and the affected lives—sometimes in very consequential ways.

Anthropologists have taught us how to best understand and evaluate who we are and who we want to become.

Participation and engagement with stakeholders—who have skin in the game—make all of the difference. All of these folks plan to live in this new community in Vancouver, BC.

1+1=3. I have an idea, and you have an idea, but the third idea that we come up with together is the best one. From overarching goals—like living lightly on the planet—to minute details—like how big the BBQ should be—these discussions are all important. It's a responsive process, it's efficient, and it generates clarity and, ultimately, community.

See the book Cohousing Communities: Designing for High-Functioning Neighborhoods to see the benefits of a deliberate process.

Goals for the Common Facilities

Imagine it is a Saturday morning in 2025 and you are sitting in the Common House reading your newspaper, and waiting for the rest of the landscape committee to arrive. You muse for a few moments how this Common House really meets previously stated goals.

What are those stated goals?

- Really inviting
- Accepting
- High degree of trust
- Invites a wide variety of life
- Comfortable alone or with others
- Emphasises the positive
- Sense of ownership

Clear agreements and documents come out of the deliberate process.

For programming to be successful, the architect must go through a detailed list of criteria with the client and look for programming needs that translate into square footage and many other design requirements. One of the most critical programming processes happens in hospital design; the plasma supply must be next to the emergency operating rooms. Programmatic hospital documents are usually 5" thick. The community programs should be at least ½" thick—the issues are really no less critical when you consider a warming planet, loss of habitats, and personal health issues, like loneliness.

The Cohousing Company's programming process includes three important steps, which are:

1. Goals
Imagine it is a beautiful morning three years from now, and you're walking from your house up to the common house. You are going to join half a dozen people on the landscape committee; the agenda is to get ready for winter (clean out drains, etc.). With coffee cup in hand, you walk up to the common terrace and think to yourself:

Wow! We did it!

We optimally satisfied our goals. I didn't get everything I wanted as an individual, but as a group, we couldn't have done better. And together, we achieved so much more than I could have ever done alone.

What are those goals?

The number usually ranges from 30 to 50, and they are agreed upon during 30 minutes of conversation.

2. Activities
What are the activities that serve your goals? What are the activities that you imagine your future neighborhood, your future common house, and your future homes to generate? Who is participating in those activities? At what time of the day, month, and year do those activities take place? Do they need their own specific places, or can they share the space with other activities?

What are those activities?

There are typically 100–150 that are consented to during a half-day workshop.

3. Places
What are the places and rooms we want on our site, in our common house, and in our homes? What kind of activities happen there? What are the characteristics of each room? Are they warm, inviting, and comfortable? How many people can each space host? Can the lighting be adjustable? What kind of furniture are we putting in each space? Where are these spaces located in relation to other spaces? And what key details do we have to consider to make these places just right?

Only after *Goals, Activities*, and *Places* are considered in great detail can you start the design process. When you thoroughly consider all significant design criteria on the front end, you will carry that knowledge and information through the subsequent design phases. This will ensure that the physical design optimizes the resources available to promote quality lives for future residents and can also provide a supportive work environment for potential staff.

The Importance of Places

A functional community behaves much like a functional family. As with a family, the dining table, the back deck, the kitchen, and the living room are central to enabling a sense of togetherness. A family struggles to thrive and grow closer together when there are no *Places* to be together; and a community is the same. Community requires a commodious *Place*. People need to have a *Place* to sit down and chat for a community to exist; the physicality must be designed into it.

The *Place* has to be inviting, attractive, and comfortable; it is essential to a functional town—or community—as much as a police department or parking enforcement. For a town to be a community, the streets have to be more than thruways. There must be eddies: places to stop and listen. This is where the whitewater gives way to a place to rest, to be, to reach out, to hear, to belong, to identify with, and to share stories. This is how a town becomes a true community to those who call it home. Public spaces have to be more inviting than a couch and TV—more appealing than digital devices. Spaces must have the additional responsibility of helping to stitch us back together into a healthy society. These better-designed spaces *can* effectively support and give back to the people who invest in their creation.

See the book Cohousing Communities *for the complete story of how to plan and design a new project for 40–50 residents at a time.*

"Give me a place that helps me grow, that cultivates both my relationships and my curiosities. Give me a place where I have as much community as I want and as much privacy as I want every day of my life."

Village Life in the 21st Century

Living a More Connected and Compassionate Life Through Environmental Design

What we have come to know as the standard forms of housing—single-family homes in suburban sprawls and monolithic housing projects in urban plots—no longer address the needs of many people. Family, community, and a sense of belonging are things that people once took for granted, but now they must be actively sought out.

There have been various proven housing and neighborhood design models—including cohousing communities and ecovillages—that reestablish many of the advantages of traditional villages within the context of 21st-century life. Family, community, a sense of belonging, respect, and accountability are sorely missing in our current social environments but can be achieved through intentional participatory design. This is particularly important in the context of neurodivergent populations, including those composed of people with autism, Down syndrome, and other neurological disorders that greatly need these social supports. None of the single-family houses or institutions that they reside in currently provide them with adequate support.

When buildings are clustered together, they create walkable streets that lead to close and meaningful destinations. Walkable streets and well-designed buildings create a series of interstitial outdoor rooms where traditional village life can manifest. Instead of having a series of garage doors, hedges, fences, or parking lots facing each other on car-dominated streets, walkable streets in clustered housing developments are fronted by lively porches and balconies, beautiful flowers and fruit trees, and collections of personal items that define the characteristics of each house's inhabitants.

People relate to one another physically and emotionally on a horizontal level. The village develops eye-to-eye relationships that not only create safer environments but also encourage people to walk, talk, and socialize with one another. The walkways become social places and playgrounds for kids and adults alike. One can sit on their front porch and chat with neighbors passing by, all while watching the visiting grandkids play. One can also knock on their neighbor's window to ask for a cup of flour or a stick of butter without driving anywhere. A sense of place emerges when there is life between the buildings. This is why one should make housing feel like an ensemble, a collection, a village instead of a strung-out and dissonant suburb, campus, or institution.

In clustered housing and village settings, buildings are generally smaller than typical suburban single-family homes. These small-sized homes lend themselves to the nature of a traditional village setting, as most villages tend to grow one small building at a time. This organic growth creates a sense of closeness that is more intimate but is not claustrophobic. It's a design that respects and enhances both community life and personal privacy.

A village has texture, varied colors, detailed nuance, and very few "missing teeth." There are no blank walls, no parking lots, no hedges, no overly large setbacks, and no vignettes devoid of interest. A village has places along the way for people to sit and contemplate and to commune. Laced with lanes, alleys, crescents, eddies (wide spots in the lane with seating, a sandbox, or a picnic table), and even basins here and there where clusters of people can gather—this is what makes a village desirable. A village feels like a village. *There is simply nothing else like it.*

A village feels like a village.

Sólheimar's aerial illustration.

Sólheimar's Architecture and Lessons Learned: Site Plan

Sólheimar has the added advantage of village-esque-ness because it prioritizes mixed-use design. On-site, there is a post office, a used bookstore, a café, a grocery store, a theater, workplaces, a woodshop, sports facilities, farming spaces and farm buildings, administration buildings, and housing for the 100+ people who live there.

This village, however, matured during the advent of cars and suffered the same affliction and addiction of too many towns where the "luxury" of being spread out turned out to be a liability. Inevitably, the day came when they realized that they were too dispersed and there were too many automobiles. Intentionality is an important implementation for organic growth in the modern age.

Sólheimar's building layout (site plan) is as organic as one might expect for a village that matured over the span of 90 years. The buildings are sporadically dispersed over about 37 acres (14.9 hectares) of land, which not only results in a confusing site plan but also in a superfluous amount of asphalt, parking lots, and roads that seemingly necessitate driving. For environmental costs, maintenance costs, and water/snow management reasons, The Cohousing Company tries to limit asphalt and gravel drive/parking areas to less than 500 square feet of area per dwelling unit in our community designs. Sólheimar has more than 2,000 square feet of driving area per dwelling, which results in more area being devoted to roads than to buildings. Villages need to be engineered and programmed carefully from the beginning to ultimately culminate in a high-quality way of life. Outdoor areas must have a distinctive sense of *Place* and definition.

If you are going to design a village like Sólheimar today, you want to consciously pursue a physical layout that doesn't resemble suburban sprawl. Suburbs are too auto-oriented, and this necessitates frequent driving—putting pedestrians in peril, especially when the roads are icy (as they often are in Iceland). A village should not resemble a college campus either, in order to avoid an institutional feel.

When Sólheimar started, Sesselja thought first and foremost that "these kids need space—they need room to roam." That's the best they could do to care for children—especially children with mental disabilities. "Let's create space;" she asked her father to help her find acreage, and he obliged.

The early residents, most of them child orphans when they moved in, are adults in their 70s and 80s, and the last thing they need is isolation. For the community to foster true independence for its residents and achieve ecological stability, it would need to abandon its reliance on cars.

Energy efficiency is easier to achieve with adjoined walls. Adjoined buildings can also be more interesting, much less costly to build, and leave less residual space. Space with no coherency, definition, or clear use only separates people from one another.

Carbon Footprint by Aurora Kuczek

One thing that became a problem for me as an environmentalist was that when I walked up and down the hill to and from class, there would be cars driving up and down those same hills. It took me about two minutes to walk from building to building. I understand if the visitors or residents need to transport loads of material to a building, but usually, it's just themselves who need to transport it across less than a half mile. It seemed very odd to me. Sólheimar was already spaced out—buildings up on the hill, houses spread all over—but it was not so spaced out that one needed to drive themselves everywhere. That carbon footprint must be very large, considering how many cars I hear from my window.

Just because you have the real estate doesn't mean you have to use it all. When long-term affordability becomes a theme, infill (structures created to fill spaces between preexisting buildings) will become a criterion. And with that infill comes more people-scaled places and fewer auto-scaled places. The worst part of spreading the buildings out like this is the loss of community that ensues. The second worst part is the cost required to outfit each building with the essentials—roads, water, sewer, electricity, etc.

Walking around Sólheimar can sometimes be a challenging task due to the lack of proximity.

The resident postman delivering the mail.

A livable village doesn't just happen by accident in the 20th and 21st centuries. Instead, it must be created through a deliberate process. For example, an essential aspect of architecture that is often overlooked, especially for the neurodivergent population, is the life between the buildings. A decorated front porch where guests, friends, and family are invited is a much more respectful segue to a private abode than plain asphalt leading to the front door. Therefore, an institution like Sólheimar will have to decide how it wants to, hopes to, and plans to grow. There is enough room between current buildings for new buildings to be constructed as infill and achieve all of the texture and color without adding the extra expense of land costs. All of the buildings now have plenty of character and nuance—the only problem is that they are too spread out and, therefore, don't have the connected coherency that you'd hope to find in a village.

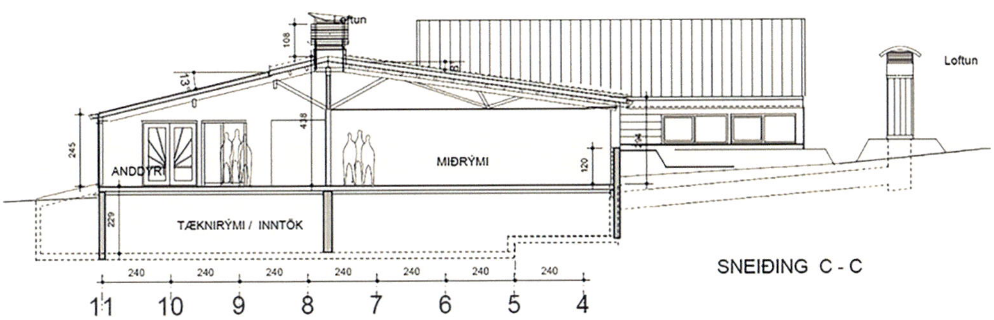

Cross section through the lobby and interstitial space, showing roof ventilation system.

COMMON FACILITIES IN SÓLHEIMAR

1. Sesseljuhús Environmental Center

Sesseljuhús is an educational center focusing on environmental issues and sustainable building techniques. It is dedicated to general education and activities that raise awareness about the environment. Courses for American students and for students at Kerhólsskóli, the school at Borg, have also been held there, along with other educational events.

Sustainable material choices like a green roof and wood.

Seminars, meetings, and workshops are held, and everyone is welcome to attend. Each summer, an exhibition on environmental issues is hosted in collaboration with Sólheimar's "Cultural Festival" (Menningarveisla), and educational materials are published.

Warm and inviting interior.

Green Buildings in Sólheimar

Sólheimar's Sesseljuhus Environmental Center is made entirely free of PVC. The wood on the building is driftwood. The paint is made from organic vegetable oils, and the walls are insulated by Icelandic wool. The ceilings are made from recycled paper.

This building is the site of many retreats that come to visit, as well as school groups who come to learn. Sesseljuhus has an environmental library inside, organized by various environmental topics related and non-related to Iceland.

Many of the buildings in Sólheimar have turf roofs. This is a very environmentally friendly option compared to a standard roof. The turf allows for rainwater catchment and reduces runoff to the surrounding areas.

2. Vigdísarhús

Vigdísarhús is an office space and community house that hosts special events such as birthdays, a Christmas buffet, and *Þorrablót* (Icelandic midwinter celebration). Activities of all types go on in Vigdísarhús, but many accentuate food production. *Vigdísarhús* also used to be the main dining hall for the villagers.

Sólheimar staff does claim, however, that they do not use this building much, as most of the common meals are hosted in *Græna Kannan*, which is conveniently located in the center of the village. This can be interpreted as the result of poor programming, where the function of the building and its relationship to other uses on the site have not been well thought out.

3. Íþróttaleikhús

Íþróttaleikhús (sports theater) is the gymnasium where morning meetings are held, as well as the theater production in the spring. Those who come are those who want to get the word out about something. As with ancient tribal traditions, making announcements does not depend on functioning internet or being tech-savvy.

For 94 years, it has been about who shows up physically to make an announcement, and then word of mouth spreads. It reminds me of how the Iroquois used to manage their six tribes.

4. Óla-smiðja

Óla-smiðja is the candle and wood workshop. Please see Chapter 4: Productivity, Pride, and Purpose for the more detailed story of how *Óla-smiðja* provides space for the residents to not only engage in the village's sustainable efforts but also to find their own sense of purpose through creation.

5. Ingustofa

Ingustofa (living room) is the second workshop, divided into art, textile, ceramics, and soap-making areas.

6. Sólheimahús

Sólheimahús was the first house built in Sólheimar in 1930. The attic of this house was where Sesselja, the founder of Sólheimar, resided from 1930 until her death.

7. Ægirsbúð

Ægirsbúð is the current administration building, located right next to the Sólheimahús Museum.

8. Græna Kannan

Græna Kannan is the café where the community has lunch. Please see Chapter 2: Sólheimar Today for the detailed story of how residents use this space to not only have their meals together but also to chat, relax, and connect with one another.

Gathering nodes, stores, and gallery spaces of residents' arts.

9. Vala Store/Gallery

Vala is the store/gift shop/gallery space right next to the Græna Kannan café.

The gallery space features art made by the residents of Sólheimar—providing a glimpse into the village's culture and creativity.

The gift shop beautifully displays sustainable artworks by the villagers, including ceramics, textiles, paintings, candles, wood sculptures, and so much more.

Due to the remote location of Sólheimar, Vala also stocks many things that one can find in a typical grocery store, from condiments to packaged food to toiletries. It also features fresh produce from the village, including tomatoes and greens harvested from the garden.

Additionally, there is a sitting nook at the end of the store where residents and visitors can come to relax and have conversations with their peers after meals in the *Græna Kannan* café.

The single place of worship where prayer is open to all.

10. Church
Everyone, regardless of their religious beliefs, is welcome in the Sólheimar Church. The church was consecrated by Rev. Karl Sigurbjörnsson, the Bishop of Iceland, on July 3, 2005, shortly before the 75th anniversary of the founding of Sólheimar.

The walls are poured concrete with a turf jacket. The roof is made of timber clad with tar paper and driftwood. The structural beams in the roof are made of laminated wood. The choice of materials for the building reflects Sólheimar's policy of using environmentally friendly materials.

The church seats 168 people on the ground floor; upstairs, there is room for 26, making the total capacity 194.

The church was financed through the Sólheimar Support Fund by monetary donations and contributions of materials from individuals and companies. It was debt-free on the day of consecration.

The single place of worship where prayer is open to all.

Permaculture is at the heart of Sólheimar and is the pride of the local residents.

The garden is a healing spot for the residents of Sólheimar.

11. Tröllagarðurinn

Tröllagarðurinn (direct translation: Giant Troll Garden) is the main outdoor garden of Sólheimar, which incorporates permaculture principles. At the opening of the gardens, a naming competition was held, and the residents chose the name Tröllagarður. Residents are encouraged to come work in the garden. Working in the garden is a fascinating and nourishing job in Sólheimar, as the villagers get a chance to pick herbs, beans, salad greens, and tomatoes for dinner. During the summer, these vegetables are also used for guests' meals.

The garden has flowers, paths, raised beds, benches, fireplaces, poetry, artwork, fairies, and other features that make working there very enjoyable. The garden is open to everyone and is used as a healing spot for the residents of Sólheimar.

The garden is now flourishing like never before and plays a big part in the beauty of Sólheimar. The garden was initiated by Valgeir Backman, who still oversees the design and organization of *Tröllagarðurinn* as well as the employees of the gardening center *Sunna* and *Sesseljuhús*.

Waste Management in Sólheimar

Water
Sólheimar recycles its own wastewater and treats the water entering through organic sewer systems. The village uses constructed wetlands that mimic the processes of natural wetlands, implementing the same flora that aid filtration in the wild. It uses a sewage separation system to sort and decompose the materials that flow into the system. Residents and visitors are strongly encouraged to use all-natural and low-impact body products while in the village. The herb workshop creates its own body products from herbs grown in the village.

Recycling
The village is very focused on recycling. Every building has organized recycling bins for plastic items, paper and cardboard, aluminum and other types of metal, and glass. In every building at Sólheimar, one can also find small, green compost waste bins lined with compostable bags. Some of the food waste goes to the greenhouse and forestry department for fertilization of the soil.

Workshops
Some of the workshops recycle old products to make new products for economic benefit. Old candles are melted to create new candles in the candle-making workshop. Old clothing is used to make rugs in the weaving workshops. Other discarded materials and fabrics can be repurposed to sew new items.

Bláskógar—the nursing care center where residents have lived for the longest and know each other like family.

Brautarholt—resident centers.

Sérbýli—the most common type of staff housing.

RESIDENTIAL BUILDINGS IN SÓLHEIMAR

The 45 residential units are for people with disabilities. The goal is to increase and maintain the residents' skills and independence and provide individualized services. There are three main types of housing, which include:

Cohabitation (*Sambýli*)
This includes *Steinahlíð*, which houses four people, and Bláskógar, where nine of the oldest residents live.

Residential Centers (*íbúðakjarnar*)
This type of housing provides private apartments for each individual resident, which includes *Brautarholt* with three bedrooms, *Sumarhús* with three rooms, and *Fagrabrekka* with two individual rooms, shared service space, and one room for a staff member.

Independent Housing (*Sérbýli*)
This is the most common type of housing for staff and "home people"—most of the units have an area of 50 square meters.

The Importance of Thorough Programming

Brautarholt—resident centers.

The difficulty for most architects in designing community housing is that they often don't see the complexities. The number one "complexity" is about achieving community in each common setting.

During my Sólheimar visit, I noticed that the kitchen (pictured left) in a shared house was not designed for cooperative cooking. Too often, five different people cook their own dinners simultaneously—and it's not designed for that. The kitchen on the right, located in another cohousing community, is designed for optimum community and cooperation. There is either an island or a table in the middle of the kitchen designed for communal cooking.

Well-designed kitchens in a shared house should include an island as a centripetal center that allows people from different households to face each other while cooking. This mitigates bumping into each other and allows for healthier interactions that are not frustrating due to cramped space.

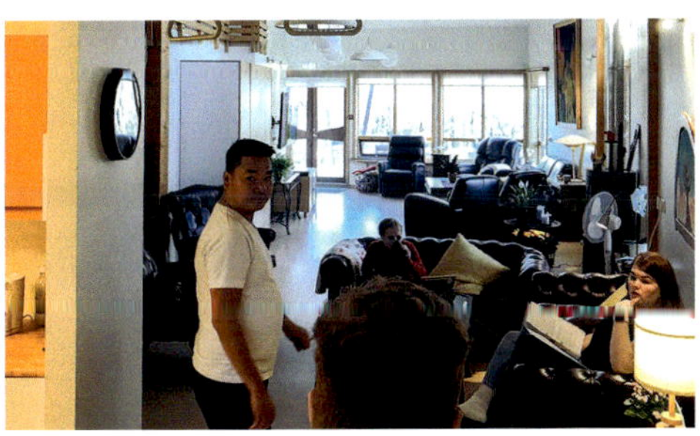

1. Bláskógar, Nursing Care

There are two "cohabitation" or "coliving" buildings: Steinahlíð and Bláskógar. Nine people live in Bláskógar; these are the residents who have lived here the longest and know each other like family. See Chapter 5.

2. Steinahlíõ

Four people live in the shared house *Steinahlíð*.

3. Sumarhús, Brautarholt, and Fagrabrekka

Sumarhús, Brautarholt, and *Fagrabrekka* are in the same category of "residential centers," where the residents have their own individual rooms, and there is a common room in the center. *Sumarhús* and *Brautarholt* each have three rooms, while *Fagrabrekka* has two rooms for residents and one room for a staff member.

A shared house with four bedrooms—one for a counselor.

Besides the four bedrooms, there are a couple of bathrooms, a kitchen, and a dining and living area.

4. Sérbýli (Independent Housing)

Sérbýli would translate as independent housing. This is the most common kind of housing: apartments, usually around 500 square feet; some are up to 850 square feet, and a couple of houses are over 1,000 square feet.

5. Upphæðir (Semi-detached Housing)

Upphæðir is the name of the semi-detached housing, categorized as independent housing.

There are about 120,000 square feet of housing in total for the 100 residents: about 1,200 square feet of housing per resident (this includes shared spaces). All employees share kitchens, dining and living rooms, and independent apartments and housing are provided for volunteers and guests. The guest houses are a real income driver for Sólheimar. They get a lot of visitors from around the world: friends, family, and people looking to learn.

The total housing could have been more cost-effective, considerably smaller, and provided more community and privacy if it was originally designed efficiently.

The greenhouses are the prominent builtscape here.

Planting seedlings.

New trees for Iceland.

Sometimes, the greenhouse gets out of control.

BUSINESS BUILDINGS

1. Sunna (Greenhouse)

The greenhouse works year-round to provide fruits and vegetables to Sólheimar and the surrounding island. Staff, volunteers, and home people work here to coordinate the most natural growing methods in Iceland. See Chapter 4 for more information.

Grow, grow, grow.

2. Ölur (Forestry)
Tree saplings are grown in Sólheimar to aid in the regrowth of the barren island. Government grants are given to raise the trees in Sólheimar. See Chapter 4 for more information.

Brekkukot Guest House with ten guest rooms.

Veghús Guest House with six double rooms and two apartment units.

Shared kitchen in the guesthouse.

Communal living room.

3. Brekkukot and Veghús Guesthouse

Brekkukot has ten rooms with shared bathrooms, as well as one apartment for rent. There are double and triple rooms and a fully equipped kitchen available for use.

Veghús has six double rooms with private bathrooms and two apartments for up to four people. There is a fully equipped kitchen.

OUT SUPPORTIVE BUILDINGS

1. Tómasarsmiðj

Tómasarsmiðja is the maintenance building, car shop, and storage space.

Not Pictured:

1. *Safnhugahús* is a non-insulated compost house.

2. *Hitaveituhús* is next to the hot spring, housing mechanical equipment and plumbing.

The Difference between Cohousing and Ecovillage

At Sólheimar, these two words are used interchangeably. Today, an ecovillage typically begins with functioning cohousing. Cohousing is a fundamental building block (there can be one or more cohousing communities in an ecovillage) because it encourages an extremely deliberate group process. In cohousing, everyone puts some money in early in the process and adopts a business-like, skin–in–the–game mindset. Most importantly, in cohousing, everyone agrees to a deliberate and fair process that best assures all voices are heard, and good ideas percolate to the top; everyone is looking for the best outcome, both emotionally and financially.

Sustainability

Our definition of an ecovillage, in combination with how it is defined by the Global Ecovillage Network, includes housing, commercial, education, farming, and production in the same place, and it does all of it with an eye towards social wellbeing, cultural responsiveness, ecological sensitivity, and economic sustainability. And a village—a functioning village—is where people settle together to create a functional community, where people know each other, care about each other, and support each other.

Sólheimar incorporates nature seamlessly. The environmental center is completely free of PVC, the walls are insulated with Icelandic wool, and the ceilings are made of recycled paper. Many buildings incorporate the use of turf rooftops. There are also pasture-raised chickens, greenhouses, and forest areas on site. They have constructed wetlands and recycle their own wastewater. The herb workshop produces its own body products—from herbs grown in the village—to facilitate a healthy wetland. Each building has an established recycling system and composts food waste. Much of the food waste goes to the local vegetable greenhouses and forestry as fertilizer, creating rich soil for crops and plants. There are also workshops that recycle old products; old clothes become rugs, and old candle remnants become ncw candles.

Increasingly, they are building structures in between existing buildings (called infill). This is a critical practice and will probably be increasingly incorporated into new communities as demands for staff and volunteer housing increase. This tactic will create more proximate villages where people can discuss composting, recycling, wetlands, and all the rest on the sidewalks. The best and most horizontal management happens on the sidewalks. This is all based not on policy but on relationships.

CHAPTER 4

What puts life into our step is the purposeful step—one that enriches our lives and pulls us, not pushes us into a happier future.

Productivity, Pride, and Purpose

This chapter is about the power of purpose. Purpose is an enhancement of self-worth, self-respect, and a real sense of contribution to society. "I am not here just to take up space. I am here to contribute what I can. I want to learn. I want to create." Purpose gives us the ability to achieve what we want as individuals and as a collective; it provides an opportunity to be whole, and folks with autism and Down syndrome appear to desire purpose as much as anyone else.

At Sólheimar, people do not have to work if they do not want to. But work is where purpose is, where creativity is, and where camaraderie is. And everyone knows—to different degrees—that's ultimately how we build a beautiful swimming pool and a bathhouse to go with it. That's what adults do in "the world;" they try to pull their weight. Adults want purpose for many realistic reasons. Quality-of-life amenities that make life more comfortable, more fun, more convenient, more fulfilling, and more meaningful are the results of purposeful work. "I'm striving for a better life, like everyone else in the world, but I'm accomplishing it more readily through cooperation than through competition. If *we* succeed, *I* succeed." Sólheimar is less like a summer camp than it is like a small town or village where there are a multitude of responsibilities and support systems that uphold the people who pursue their purpose through action.

People do not have to work, but this is a good place to go if you do want to. People who value purpose often choose Sólheimar over other options. For some, it's about breaking free from a sense of stagnation and languishment—those who feel like "I've got to get out there and do something." There's no judgment here, but for many, this kind of involvement is what it takes for them to feel whole.

DOI: 10.4324/9781003642336-5

Artisanal Handicraft Workshops
Since its inception, Sólheimar has prioritized arts, handicrafts, and the use of natural resources to create valuable and beautiful objects. This instills a sense of purpose and creativity in the life of the village and the villagers.

The workshops are central to helping people learn, find purpose, grow together, and be together. Day in and day out, they feel the camaraderie and support through hours of peer interaction, learning new skills, and ultimately growing more self-confident in their abilities and social proficiencies. Over a dozen workshops help everyone explore their curiosities, discover their unique skills, contribute in their own best way, and develop in their chosen directions.

The workshop participants: weaving, sculpting clay, woodworking, and conversing. People share coffee and snacks during their morning and afternoon breaks, five days per week. The space is warm yet light and airy.

Working together makes things happen. The mentorship, the materials, the purpose—it's all there. "Let's make something beautiful today" becomes a prevailing attitude.

Ceramics

The ceramic workshop provides a space for the villagers to explore their creativity—working out basic ideas through molding, painting, glazing, and finishing. Many try their hand at different types of products—from large sculptures to small artworks, as well as practical items such as cups and bowls.

In the ceramics workshop, folks become Artisans with a capital A.

Ceramic artworks right out of the kiln.

Guðni Th. Jóhannesson, President of Iceland, visiting the ceramic workshop.

Artistic expression has a rich local tradition, and Sólheimar Art is a product of that creativity.

Erla Björk Sigmundsdóttir, born in 1973, is one of the spectacular artists who lives and works in Sólheimar. Erla found her purpose in the art workshops; her embroidery received special attention and admiration, as did her clay works based on Erla Bjarkar's drawings. Erla Björk has been invited to participate in numerous exhibitions and was chosen as an artist of Arts Without Borders in 2016. Erla's works reflect the unique power that resides within. Her figurative work is dynamic, expressive, beautiful, and highly sought after.

Kristján Atli Sævarsson (KAS), born in 1994, lives and works in Sólheimar. Kristján Atli is a versatile artist who pursues his art purposefully; he is also an active participant in Sólheimar's Theater Association. His *Rjúpan* (bird sculpture) has been very popular and repeatedly sells out in all its different forms. He has a strong sense of style; his thin brush strokes are disciplined and precise with a unique cadence that ebbs and flows.

Sólheimar and its workshops give its residents the opportunity to grow, develop, and become active participants.

Creative drawings to ceramics, and vice-versa.

Einar Baldursson (EB) moved to Sólheimar at a young age and has made a name for himself as one of the most in-demand artists of our time. Einar has received much attention and recognition; he was chosen as the artist of Art Without Borders in 2009.

Einar draws emphatically and has developed a strong personal style; he designs firmly and decisively, and his figurative drawings are lively, colorful, and descriptive. Casts of his ceramics are produced in limited editions and modeled after the artist's drawings.

Weaving
A range of woven items can be made in the weaving shop, where four large looms are used to produce floor mats, tablecloths, and textiles for bags and woolen blankets. Most of the material is recycled from old bedclothes, jeans, and knitting wool. Knitting, crocheting, and embroidery are also done in the weaving shop, and employees are welcome to create whatever they so choose with the available materials.

The tutor to the right is helping Olafur create what he desires. He wants to contribute to the craft store's success, improve his art, and be creative. There is a consequential nexus between purpose and happiness. Engaging mentorship helps to bring everyone closer to their individual goals.

Some people want to work in the large workshop group with others, and some prefer to work on their own. Community, when people want community, and privacy when they want it—that is the secret sauce. They have that choice at work and beyond; however, they gravitate more and more to community settings over time.

"How am I going to make this yarn into art?" Art is a phenomenon that some don't fully appreciate when they move into Sólheimar. Then, over time, there is a growing appreciation, understanding, and, eventually, a breakthrough.

"I've been here for a while, and I'm just becoming the artist I want to be."

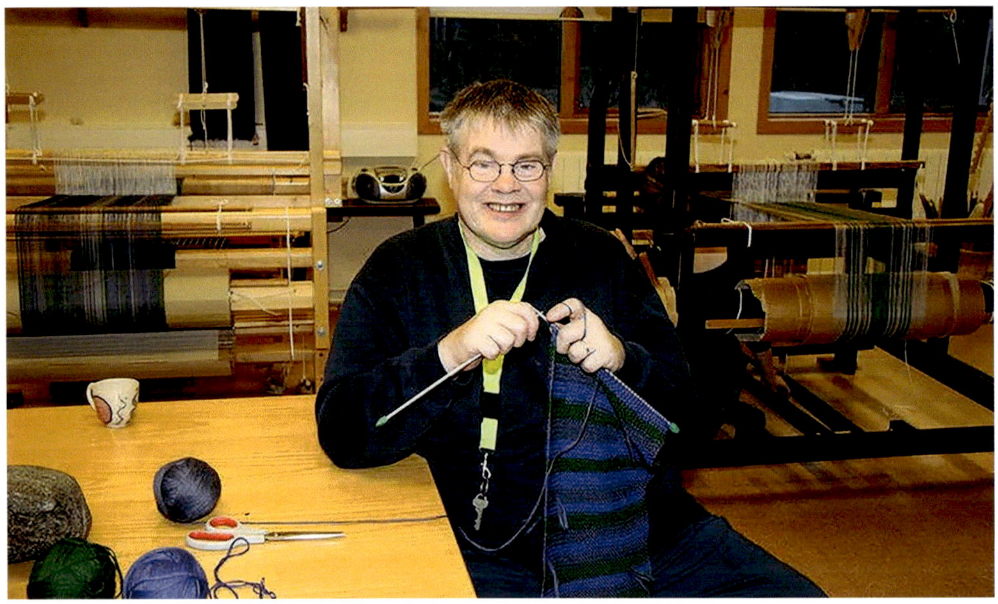

Felted tapestries made at the weaving and textiles workshop. Two-dimensional felt work is a specialty at Sólheimar. Textiles are bought as art for homes but also for offices and institutions, where art helps to mitigate acoustic reverberation in cavernous spaces, entries, and hallways. There are so many needs that are met best by folks living harmoniously with autism; focus, patience, inclination, and sensitivity are some of their strengths.

Woodworking

Sólheimar's woodworking shop produces artworks and practical items, including candlesticks, food utensils, sculptures, cabinetries, and toys. Employees of the woodworking shop also undertake various maintenance and woodworking assignments at Sólheimar. Efforts are made to use locally sourced timber when possible.

Branches to chimes that make music when the wind blows, which is frequent. Background music that is made on-site.

A community, taking their time, can fulfill the full purpose of this precious resource.

Value-added: scraps of wood transform into furniture. The making of useful things through teamwork provides gratification, purpose, and satisfaction.

Supplies adorn the walls in the woodcraft areas.

Value-added wood from pruning and clearing trees—often donated and, on occasion, purchased from a local wood vendor—is turned into products at the Sólheimar workshop. From sticks to candle holders, children's toys, Christmas decorations and more—creativity here is abundant.

Value-added wood turned to playful sculpture. These are always in demand at the Sólheimar store.

These residents are becoming artisans through their daily work. Their creations sell well at the common store and online.

(Left) Donated wood turned into crafts that help the community afford some of their needs. Creative woodworking projects like this musical instrument are made in the wood shop.

(Right) Value added: taking free scraps of wood from a construction site, gluing and screwing them together—this makes great corbels for various construction projects that would cost $200–300 each to build from scratch. Value-adding keeps the costs down. Getting construction off-cuts for free and putting them on the lathe can lead to sculpture.

Candle-Making

The candle-making workshop provides the space for residents to handcraft their very own unique candles from beeswax (for indoor uses) and recycled candle wax and candle stubs (for outdoor uses).

Over and over again, home people become masters of their chosen trade. Whether they're making candles, candle holders, wax colorations, or other crafts, they become true artisans.

The love warmth and glowing light; candles have historically been a means of making money for Sólheimar. Making candles seems to be very gratifying for all parties, including the consumers.

It turns out there are a lot of ways to make a candle, as well as many ways to hold it. The visitors of Sólheimar appreciate them enough to buy them, order them online, and love having them on their dining table, just like I do!

Beeswax candles—one of hundreds of value-added products produced at Sólheimar—are popular. Everyone loves them, and Sólheimar residents are quite adept at rolling them into the perfect form.

Candles that I bought at Sólheimar provide the light that soothes and warms me at my table in California. I sat and watched the creation of these candles. They took about 2½ minutes each to complete the final rolling step and provoked smiles from the workers and the observers alike. It reminded me of watching artisan cigar makers in Latin America.

Art Workshops

The Sólheimar art workshop is where the villagers can explore their creativity through a variety of mediums and create both decorative and practical items. They create artwork in various forms through watercolor painting, embroidery, beading, wool felting, pencil drawing, ceramics, and more.

Each craft room or workshop (for ten or so people) has a break room where they have a morning snack and an afternoon coffee or tea together. In these rooms, the warmth and natural light, the acoustics, and the proximities are just right; the chairs are comfortable, and you feel the love and friendship present in the space.

This is the concept of *hygge*. You'll hear institutions say, "Oh, we can't afford to do that." I argue that cultivating a comfortable environment and a sense of *hygge* can be inexpensive and is among the most worthwhile things you can invest in for individual and collective comfort and the long-term productivity of all. In fact, you truly can't afford not to implement *hygge*!

The workshops help everyone explore their curiosities, find their unique skill, contribute in their best way, grow in their chosen directions, and develop meaningful relationships that last a lifetime.

(Left) Organizing beads for a new project. Some crafts are very straightforward. Organizing beads in a bowl, for example, is a Montessori-like task. It is also a good activity for a relaxing day and for a person with an abundance of patience—which this woman has.

(Right) Art projects like this bead art don't require many large tools or equipment. These projects can also be done in a leisurely manner in the dining room at Sólheimar nursing care.

(Top Left) Sunny coffee break and snack room. One of these exists for every couple of workshops.

(Top Right) Some people like to work alone, and some prefer to work alongside others. Preferences ebb and flow; the important thing is to accommodate all moods and provide the best of both worlds. Most people choose to work with others.

(Bottom Left) Painting and tapestry made by the residents of Solheimar.

Pharmaceutical

Pharmaceutical companies employ some residents here for their sorting skills, and this has proven to be symbiotic. I was told that the companies pay top rates to Sólheimar hires because they want to support the community. Sólheimar considerably enhances the pharmaceutical ability to recycle and avoid landfills.

Liselotte Hyveled, who started the program "Including the Excluded" at the pharmaceutical company Novo Nordisk, makes it her mission to provide purpose for folks with autism.

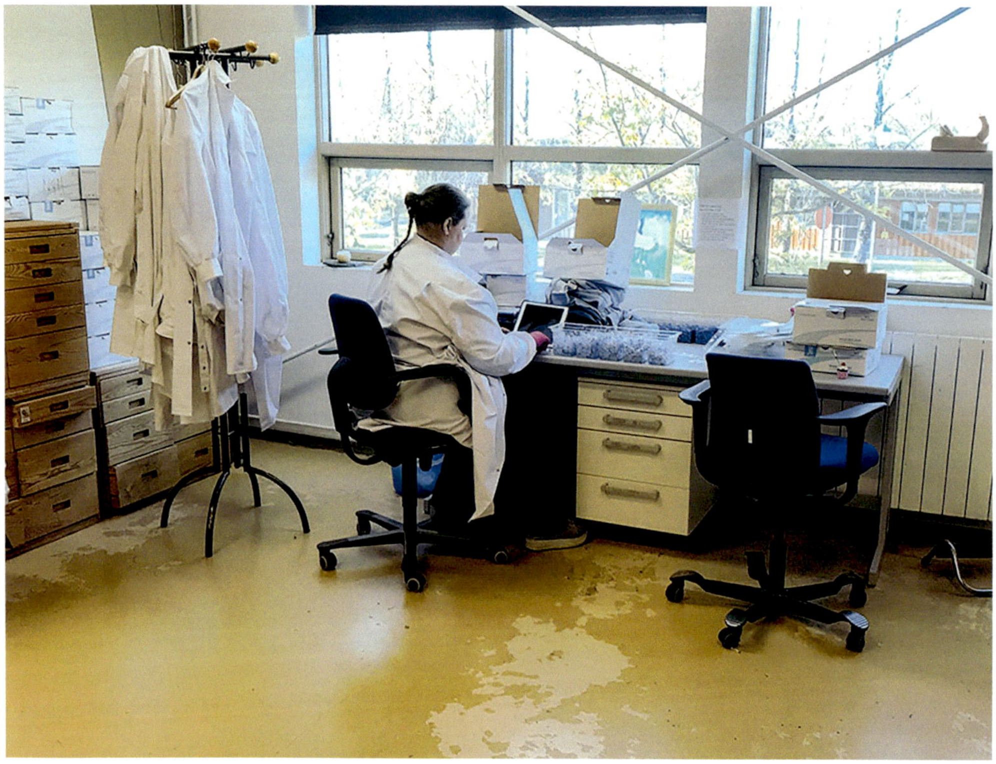

Pharmaceutical companies have hired Sólheimar residents to do careful sorting—a tedious and meticulous skill enjoyed by many people with autism.

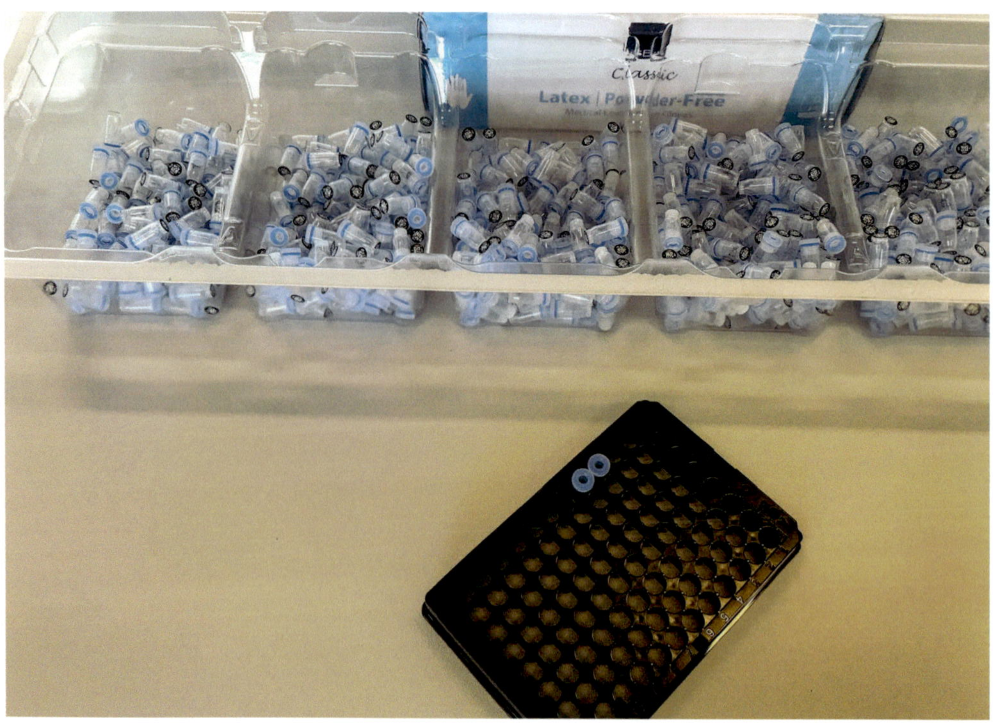

Patient, organized, and careful work is the trick—embodying Mari Montessori's philosophy. This can be hard for some people when the work is extremely repetitive, but there are many in the autistic community for whom this is enjoyable.

The Vegetable Greenhouses at the "Sunna Horticultural Center" *(Garðyrkjustöðin Sunna)*

The Sunna Horticultural Center is considered the cradle of organic farming in Iceland, as it is generally believed that the origin of modern organic farming in the Nordic countries exists here at Sólheimar. Sesselja was a great lover of nature and cared deeply about environmental issues. The focus on organic agriculture and lifestyle is core to the appeal of Sólheimar, and it attracts volunteers from around the world.

Endless greenhouses are the future of agriculture in cold climates, providing food security, good local and organic food, and maintaining a smaller carbon footprint.

These greenhouses were a brilliant investment for Sólheimar, allowing them to produce food year-round. Greenhouse gardening is the epitome of the Montessori philosophy: every job can be bifurcated, trifurcated, and subdivided into components that are easy to understand and implement.

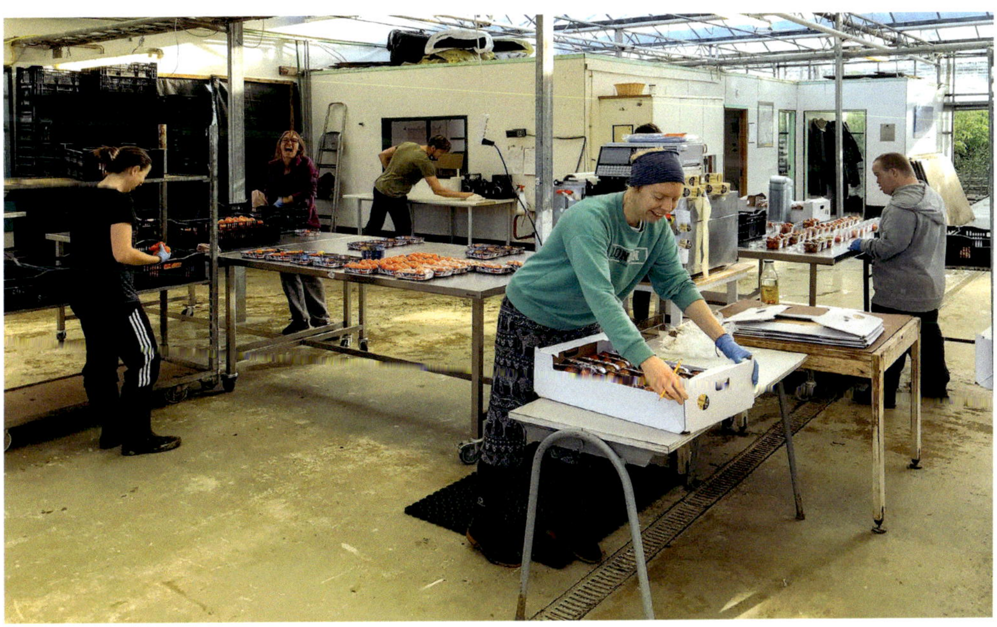

Purpose, friends, music, food, interests that fulfill curiosities, getting better at all of it, and getting paid: these elements are at the core of getting things done and setting the community up for success. "If we do this and this, the tomatoes are redder, tastier, grow faster, and so on. . . . If we plant now, use this soil, and water this often, these peppers should grow better." A director, several volunteers, and lots of home people are involved in these processes.

The greenhouses are very organized; it's easy for skilled and non-skilled people to plug in. There is ample space for innovation and growth in the greenhouses, and there are constantly evolving technologies and management strategies. The Sunna Center provides considerable training both for residents and outside volunteers. The greenhouses facilitate community; while some of the work is individual, most of it is done in a group setting. It is a great place to work while volunteers, staff, and residents get to know each other. Inside the greenhouse is a dry, warm, windless environment—an ideal working place in Iceland during the winter. It's very comforting; people look at each other and talk to one another to get things done.

The forestry greenhouse for starter plants: new to Sólheimar, but an advantageous addition for them and for Iceland. Tree saplings are grown in Sólheimar to aid in the growth of the barren island. Government grants are given to raise the trees at Sólheimar.

An abundance of food protected from the frost and the elements. Some gardens are outside, but the most productive ones are in greenhouses.

"Look what we've accomplished here:" the greenhouses at work. They have saved considerable costs to Sólheimar, and the fresh food provides satisfaction for residents and volunteers from around the world who are motivated to learn how Sólheimar works. These volunteers contribute to a clear solution for the population of Sólheimar and are motivated to see "exotic" Iceland.

Indoor vertical greenhouses grow an abundance of food without costly and complicated structures because the food and the interior framework are protected from the wind. When crops are outside, vertical growing is limited.

Vertical plants protected from the wind produce much more food per square meter.

Greenhouses in Colder Climates Are the Future of Local Food

The greenhouses are great for keeping food production and resources local. As of 2023, Sunna's main products include tomatoes, eggplants, small cucumbers, celery, brussels sprouts, cauliflower, broccoli, chilies, melon, corn, beans, onions, squash, pumpkins, potatoes, kiwi, salad greens, herbs like parsley, rosemary, basil, coriander, and lavender. Not having these goods imported from Southern Europe, South America, Israel, or elsewhere means transportation costs and carbon footprint are lower. The produce grown here is not designed for shipping around the world but is rather designed for flavor—and it's noticeable.

(Top) Sometimes, the "garden" goes crazy in the greenhouse. That's pretty much the opposite of what's going on outside in the sparse lava fields.

(Left) Fresh produce used in the village's canteen and sold at the village's store.

Abundance flourishes for folks who grew the food themselves, take pride in it, sell it, and consume it. People who work to grow their own food (and know they grew what they're consuming) feel better about themselves.

The amount of food the Sunna Center provides is considerable: it accounts for about 50% of all the vegetables and fruit consumed in the village. They sell back to the on-site village store (Völu) and village canteen for common lunches as well as the Samkaup/Netto stores in bigger cities like Reykjavík. They create a revenue of about 300–500 thousand ISK ($2,215–$3,685) per week from Samkaup/Netto and around 3 million ISK ($22,150) annually from the village's kitchen and store. Sunna is also planning to have more residents of Sólheimar work at the center and intends to become more sustainable by prioritizing the fruits and vegetables for the Sólheimar kitchen while relying less on selling to stores in Reykjavik. This will also minimize the food waste in the village.

The costs to run the greenhouse every year—including water, fertilizer, heat, electricity, staff (mostly residents and volunteers), maintenance, supplies, and financing—and the revenue that it generates have about evened out over the past several years. It is also important to consider the costs that the greenhouse saves Sólheimar by having food produced on-site instead of being bought and transported.

Given a job to do at the greenhouse, Reynir can be productive for hours, taking the weeds out of the compost or other straightforward jobs. Then he does another job after that. Seven-hour workdays, five days per week. A morning of working and communing with friends and an afternoon of hiking and fellowship with friends—makes for a full life. Living well and with purpose makes for a full life.

State-of-the-art greenhouses make things happen.

International volunteers and home people prepare the plant starts.

The Forestry Center/Tree Nursery (*Skógræktin Ölur*)

The Forestry Center is essential to Sólheimar; founded in 1991, it started as one of the first tree farms on the island of Iceland. The Ölur Center produces trees for forestry on Sólheimar's own land (they maintain 494 acres or 200 hectares) and sells to the public and to landscape and government companies. They are also successfully increasing tree production by working with the Forestry Agency in Iceland, as well as with companies that need genuine carbon offsets.

Each year, they grow thousands of seedlings from a variety of species, including Sitka Spruce, Aspen, Fir, Black and Red Alder, and others. At a couple of hundred thousand dollars in both revenue and cost per year, the tree farm currently breaks about even but will likely be profitable soon.

Excess carbon in the atmosphere, in combination with deforestation, is a global problem. We must stop the carbon bleeding into the atmosphere; carbon sequestering is an important solution to the real-world problem of climate change. There will need to be considerable removal/sequestering of carbon in the near future using methods such as machine technology and regenerative agriculture—where farms put less carbon into the atmosphere by ceasing to use fossil fuels and keeping CO2 embedded in the soil.

We can slow the progress of climate change by generating more oxygen, protecting and creating animal habitats, and protecting watersheds. The simplest and best way to accomplish this is through reforestation and continuously planting a multitude of trees.

Our arboreal friends are the lungs of the planet: the work that occurs at the Ölur Forestry Center is, therefore, one of the noblest types of work that can be done.

Trees, trees, trees. Residents of Sólheimar are taking their forestry practices to the next level and are growing to sell every tree to forestry departments, businesses, and individuals who want to remove carbon dioxide from the atmosphere.

The prevailing feeling inside the greenhouse is abundance above scarcity.

(Left) Seedlings galore, to be used at Sólheimar and sold to the public.

(Right) The new tree greenhouse/forestry seedling nursery. Sólheimar has a new effort of consequence: to start tree seedlings on site. The seedlings later get replanted nationwide to help absorb greenhouse gases and provide windbreaks, among countless other benefits.

Relative to other countries, Iceland has few trees because soil production and build-up are slow: not enough birds leave their seed-rich guano here. As a result, most of the wood required to build and take care of existing buildings is currently imported. Sólheimar is the perfect place for starting new trees to both plant all over the country and provide material for large new timber buildings.

With guidance from the director, Eiður Eyþórsson, volunteers and residents work together at the Forestry Center. Although the scope of work is immense and must be meticulously organized, when broken up into smaller tasks, this type of work can be meditative and calming. For example, residents gently pull apart the tender seedlings from their starting pack—taking care not to rip the fragile roots—and transplant them into their own cells to grow into strong saplings. It's a very peaceful scene: the gentle pitter-patter of rain on the roof and soft light filtering in, the entire floor of the 8,000 square foot greenhouse is carpeted in vibrantly verdant little seedlings. It's a nursery for future gentle giants that will one day provide us and subsequent generations with the air we need to breathe. That's something to be incredibly proud of fostering.

Note from Eiður, the Director of Ölur Forestry Center

The main purpose of the Ölur is to accelerate the reforestation in Iceland. Growing and planting trees is what we do. It's an immense undertaking to forest the island; we may only play a small role in that. However, every step taken in the right direction is a step worth taking, as Iceland is now a bit of a lavascape.

The best part about this job is the privilege of working in the service of nature, knowing that the more you do, the greater the positive impact will be in the future. One cannot be anything but grateful to be able to busy oneself with meaningful work with a strong purpose: one that is not merely self-serving but is serving on a level that encompasses all life.

On the nation-serving level, it is no less crucial that we rebuild the forests. Iceland has been poor for most of the time, but it has been settled: it's only been a few decades since things really began to change for the better, which means that now we have a window, however brief or long it may be. People are not forced to busy themselves with survival alone but have the luxury to expand their mind's horizons and think beyond. With that also comes the benefit of thinking long-term, which is an essential part of growing forests. With the window we now have, it's paramount that we rebuild the ecosystem so that future generations will have local resources to rely on when they need them. One doesn't prepare for winter when it has arrived; that's what the other seasons are for.

In Ölur, we have a policy. Let the ones who wish to come, come. And let those leave who so wish. A project like this doesn't happen without a team effort. A healthy team is formed when everyone finds it in themselves that this is something they want to do. The passion for the work and interest in the project must be there for the willingness to do well to arise; good work will generally follow as a result. What I hope we get out of the work is what we need to learn beyond just the physical tasks at hand. Whether it may be greater patience, discipline, developing their work ethic, or a better sense of direction in life—that is the journey. In short, growing trees can also be just as much about fostering the human spirit.

The hoop house for the tree nursery.
One inspired resident sought to make his mark by cultivating tree seedlings and forest-worthy trees at Sólheimar then distributing the mature trees all over Iceland. The trees don't yet make a profit, but after just a couple of years, they almost break-even—and the future is promising.

The nursery at Sólheimar is one of the best in Iceland. Beginning with proven methods is the best way to get plants started in this basaltic soil.

A sense of purpose is what society, families, and individuals want. I see it in their eyes, and I feel it in their hearts. The difference between having and not having purpose is the difference between wanting to thrive versus not caring to thrive. Whether it's the independence, the workshops, the green shops, the tree farm, or the community, it all brings meaning to us collectively and individually.

CHAPTER 5

A house is just a shell.
A home is the relationships that we have with others inside and outside of our walls.

Nursing Care (Bláskógar)

Bláskógar is the name for the comfortable home for folks who need more or less full-time assistance (usually 24-hour care). The home provides a warm and caring place to live the last years of life as if they greatly matter because they do. It provides a place to come in for a smooth and secure landing. It feels like the antidote to an institutional setting such as a nursing home. It feels like the antidote to dying alone—like a home away from home, it is a continuation of the home and community cultivated at Sólheimar, where neighbors become friends and friends become family.

Introduction to Bláskógar, Nursing Care Home at Sólheimar
Folks grow old at Sólheimar, and that's a good thing! There is no reason to be uprooted and moved to a place where you are anonymous—surrounded and cared for by strangers. Residents and their families can expect a beautiful life ending at Sólheimar. This end-of-life support accommodates the needs that are accompanied by the realities of aging.

DOI: 10.4324/9781003642336-6

Bláskógar was built on site about 20 years ago. It is one of the two buildings in Sólheimar that is a "cohabitation/co-living" type of housing in which residents have their own room and share a kitchen and living rooms. It's where the oldest residents live. It consists of individual studio apartments for nine residents with a central shared service space. Anna Þuríður Pálsdóttir, a director at Sólheimar, says, "These are the residents that have lived here the longest—they're almost 90 years old—that know each other like family." And because of this, "the relations between residents are like in families where there is a lot of friendship and love." Many residents have lived at Sólheimar for a long time. Inevitably, one day, they need daily medical attention—this is a good time to move to Bláskógar. Most importantly, they are surrounded by people with whom they grew older in Bláskógar and in the larger village of Sólheimar. They already know the caregivers because they have visited their ailing peers there for years.

The relatively new, warm, and giving nursing care building with common dining and living spaces. There are private rooms for each of the older residents of Sólheimar. Note the grass roof.

The State of Elder Care in Our Modern World

The way elders are treated and cared for in modern society is a cause for great and widespread concern. Even with all the resources available in developed countries, almost none of them can create places where you'd want to spend the end of your life. Dr. Bill Thomas, a renowned author and eldercare activist, effectively argues that nursing care is an ill-conceived combination of a hospital and a prison. Residents are, in fact, locked in. Sólheimar offers an alternative model: multiple large and small gathering areas, stimulating home spaces allowing for conversation and activities in accordance with physical ability. All of the doors are unlocked; the residents are free.

Skilled nursing care—where residents have access to 24/7 nursing and other personal care and medications—is usually considered the last resort before hospice. Often, to make it "efficient" and cost-effective, we make it only as humane as necessary in order to comply with legal requirements. Even developed countries have extreme difficulty creating comfortable and positive nursing care environments. A woman recently described to the Scottish Parliament that in the last year, she had 133 different caregivers come to her home to provide care. That's 133 different explanations of her personal needs, which can be a very intrusive and impersonal way to "get the job done."

Personal horror stories abound too often in typical nursing care environments. The seniors are abused, and many caregivers feel abused as well. Residents may not be turned over frequently enough, not washed regularly, or not properly medicated. The environment may have an overabundance of plastic, fluorescently lit rooms, and often no choice about whether or not to have roommates. The TV is always on, isolation and unsatisfactory food abound—the list goes on and on.

When significant events such as pandemics or catastrophic natural disasters occur, the effects on the elderly are monumental. Add under-staffing and daily changes in caretakers, low wages, insufficient training, disenfranchised families, increasing dementia, language barriers, loneliness, and depression; it is a perfect storm at the very least. According to *The American Journal of Geriatric Psychiatry*, 10% of those in nursing care reported abuse. That number increased by 84% during the pandemic. This is a lose-lose situation.

A lot of older American seniors are in great despair because of this bleak situation. Suicide for men 55 and older is at an all-time high of 30 per 100,000 (CDC). Many people's worst fear is to be a body in a bed, merely kept "alive," without a real reason to keep going. My nephew Tony spent a brief period of time delivering Meals on Wheels. Many seniors would start crying when he started to leave after a mere five minutes in his company; they wanted him to stay. It was emotionally draining for everyone involved.

There are 15,600 nursing care institutions in the U.S. alone, according to the National Center for Health Statistics. No matter how hard they try to change licensing requirements or formal protocol, they absolutely cannot please everyone—least of all the human beings lying in that bed *right now*. Nursing care is not hospice, nor should it feel that way; but in fact, in our current system, it becomes so.

As of 2023, the median wage for a caregiver in the U.S. was $15.22/hour, according to the Economic Policy Institute. These low rates of pay are setting us up for failure.

There are 4,600 adult daycare services in the U.S. These are places where seniors are carted off to day care activities for the elderly. This is by necessity; we are social animals and need company at least once a day. While this "daycare" is necessary in our current system, it is in no way sustainable. These teeming buses are embarrassing for seniors as they haul them around on mandated day trips; they feel as if they're riding on school buses for children. The trips simultaneously emit large amounts of fossil fuels and contribute to environmental degradation—they are the antithesis of the community in the neighborhood.

Caregivers Need Care Too

Research shows that caregivers are at considerable risk for anxiety, depression, chronic health problems, and financial strain. With little to no government support, how can we support caregivers?

- *60% of caregivers in California show clinically significant signs of depression*
- *22% report severe loneliness*

(Source: KQED Forum episode Jan 17, 2024).

There are also 12,200 home health agencies in the U.S., amplifying estrangement and consequently neglecting emotional needs. Americans drove over 7 billion miles in 2023 to provide meals on wheels and formal home health care for seniors. In Sacramento County, California, there were 500,000 meal-related auto-trips for 4,100 seniors from one agency alone (out of 12,200 across the country). That doesn't account for the billions of miles traveled by relatives to check up on their families. These services and trips have an enormous carbon footprint and increase the risk of road fatalities. At this moment in time, these services are imperative and indeed provide essential care—but we can do better. Meals on Wheels and home health care are not the problem; they are simply a band-aid for the deeper cuts plaguing today's society. A much more sustainable and enriching way of aging is possible, and together, we need to find our way back to the values of village living.

Porch scenario at a cohousing in the U.S. Sitting outside at Bláskógar with neighbors looks something like this.

Being truly "alive" is best accomplished in a functioning village/neighborhood. There are countries around the world that are guided by communities and cultures that honor their elders and put quality of life first; they see the advantages of neighborhood-making. Neighborhood-making means creating communities that connect the population from a deep, anthropological, and compassionate perspective. It is not done by creating one more rule for nursing care facilities or a magic bullet policy—because there isn't one. It requires designing each neighborhood *with* and *for* the people who plan to live there. On average, these neighborhoods take less time and cost less to build. They are much healthier psychologically, physiologically, and environmentally.

Village Elder/Nursing Care as a Solution

> *We can't turn the clock back, but we can consciously embrace old-world village-making in contemporary society.*

What does elder care and nursing care for folks with autism and Down syndrome look like in a high-functioning village? Bláskógar serves as a successful demonstration. When aging, there is nothing better than being surrounded by folks who you've known your whole life. There is nothing like a familiar face, a familiar smile. Bláskógar is just one part of Sólheimar, but it's a critical part: the part that makes a village whole. It's the part where elders are honored and ennobled.

Giving these sage elders a noble and honored curtain call is not new technology—it's enabling opportunities for kinship by tapping into ancient wisdom. We can't turn the clock back, but we can conscientiously embrace old-world village-making in contemporary society.

There are seniors currently embracing this opportunity around the world. See The Cohousing Company's *Senior Cohousing Handbook*, which addresses Dr. Bill Thomas' comment that "you can put 20 seniors on a boat and sail them out to a desert island, and they will accomplish a setting and provide for themselves better than any institution created by all the PhD gerontologists created to date."

Aesthetics and The Built Environment of Nursing Care: Nurturing, Organic, Soft, and Warm

Sólheimar has done something to the care culture; nothing looks institutionalized. Sesselja was a fan of Rudolph Steiner, and Sólheimar is very much inspired by his design philosophy. Aesthetically, it's designed to be warm and cozy—full of *hygge*. But most importantly, it's designed to be welcoming, giving, and accommodating for physical wellbeing. The ideal room is warm, with non-fluorescent lights and considerable woodwork. The kitchen is right in the middle, generating a natural gathering point that is clad in warm wood—it's not made of cold, stainless steel. Even the baseboards are made of wood. Sesselja attempted to use wood wherever possible and avoided 90° angles; obtuse angles were interspersed here and there to enhance the homey ambiance. This warm and giving environment helps to foster long-lasting and rich relationships created over the years because it *brings people in*—you want to be in that space with others and tell tales of your former years, current years, and even the future.

Cohousing in the U.S.: dinner at Bláskógar looks something like this.

Common Areas

In Bláskógar, the common areas—like the dining room and kitchen—are residents' homes away from home. Some folks get dinner taken to their room, of course, and some make their own in their personal kitchenettes—but most eat here together. In the common kitchen, both residents and professionals cook. The key lies in making it fun and inviting for everyone—to avoid making it feel like an institution. The kitchen is the hub, just like at home. People gather, sit, talk, watch, and participate in making food if they can. This is where people live—it's their home.

The corridors are not straight: they're shaped organically (mostly obtuse angles) and are trimmed in natural wood. Everything that can be wood is wood, which helps to create an environment that does not feel institutional. There are very few ceiling-mounted fluorescent lights; the necessary artificial lighting that does exist provides a soft, warm glow (2700k), and the bulbs are all the same temperature. Natural light indoors and connection to outdoor environments play a huge role in illuminating the space and contributing to regular circadian rhythms; aspects that are often disregarded in elder care spaces but enhance wellbeing significantly. These are small details that make a big difference.

There is outside seating and a dining area with a BBQ for the warmer months, which makes the back terrace feel like a part of the great outdoors. It feels like a summer lodge in the summer and a ski lodge in the winter.

"On vacation" at Bláskógar, enjoying the outdoor patio—the general feeling is, "Why not?"

At Bláskógar, some residents get up early every morning and busy themselves. Here, a resident is sorting beads for an upcoming project.

The dining room at Bláskógar.

The common living room at Bláskógar.

A few residents and I were enjoying the living room at one point during my stay when a cat walked into the room. The conversation stopped for a moment, everyone smiled, and then we continued talking . . . moments to pause and just enjoy each other's company are frequent in Bláskógar, and Sólheimar generally.

The ambiance in the nursing care building is warm and calm.

Shared Housing/Private Room

The private rooms in Bláskógar are generously sized, furnished, and full of natural light. Yolanda (seen Figure 5.13, left) from Poland had a true personality; she kept residents and caregivers entertained and on their toes. Each resident in the nursing care facility has their own private room, bathroom, and a small kitchenette for when they're not feeling social.

The corridors are not straight and there are varied vignettes along the way.

(Left) Yolanda in her warm, private, cream-colored room. She had Down syndrome. She recently died, which was a big loss for the Sólheimar community. Her wisdom, stories, and humor entertained many for years.

(Right) In-room kitchenette, for those days that you don't feel well and just want a cup of tea.

(Left) A typical private room—awash in natural light for as much of the day as possible.

(Right) Another one of the private rooms in Bláskógar, with warm-colored paint and wooden flooring.

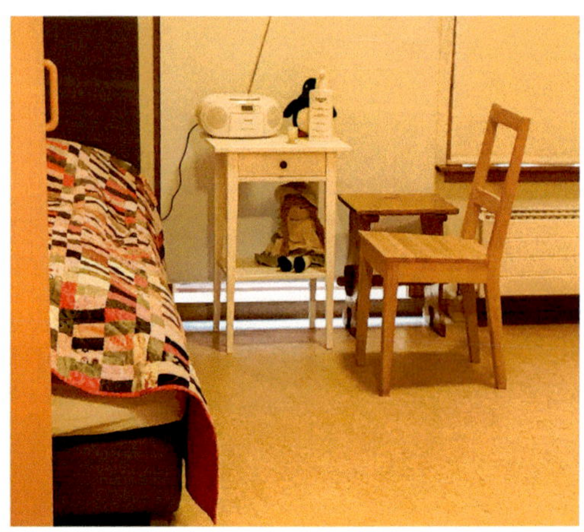

Details are sensitive to a variety of physical realities.

Putting the Care in Caregivers: The Staff at Bláskógar
Sólheimar intentionally employs dedicated staff with extensive training and qualifications. The staff here serve those with disabilities by assisting with personal care, dressing, mobility, and nursing. At night, there is always one staff member on duty at Bláskógar, and others are on-call if something comes up. Although the caregivers don't live on-site, they know all of the residents and feel accountable to them.

The staff are familiar people that the residents have known forever; they are very dedicated to showing up every day with intention and kindness. They believe in humanity for all; it's not just a job for them.

One quote I'll never forget is, "This setting allows the residents to care for each other." This is compassion. There is enduring concern: "How is she doing?" "Can I go in and read to her?" "I'd like to wash her feet—she likes that."

No institutionalized form of care has the resources or the funds to lather the love that is necessary in life's waning years; only history with others can do that.

Some of these caregivers spend their lifetime caring for others. Lots of people do this work for a living; the pull of community fosters inclusion among *all* of the residents. Caregivers know and care about the residents at Sólheimar; they support them in ways that are only possible when you feel like a family. You are one of them; you have been a part of the same village forever.

Friends and Neighbors Become a Kind of Family
Another recognizable component of wellbeing in a community is how much the residents are cared for by others and visited by friends and neighbors in the village. Many of the other residents stop by Bláskógar to check on and commune with their older friends, some of whom have been living at Sólheimar for 80 years. The quality of care received by the residents of Bláskógar is very much influenced by these visitors. In these final years, the community plays the lead role. Purpose shifts from "here are all

These needs never go away, as expressed in this poster at Bláskógar.

A young woman who works at Bláskógar. She's dedicated to helping make the waning years another fruitful component of our One Life.

A noble career: helping aging folks be at home in these cozy environs. Ingla has worked here for 12 years. Her calm and patience influence the feelings of the entire culture.

A mother-like figure is comforting and nurturing when needed and desired and is directed by the residents themselves, along with professionals. The last few years of life can be full of pain and sadness, or it can be another enriching and meaningful time that staff members help to facilitate.

the things I want to get done today" to "I have to get dressed; someone might come to visit."

There are too many seniors in the world who are abandoned to typical nursing care facilities and rarely visited by friends and family. Families might have a falling out, but more likely, they just become too busy or live too far away. This is not the case in villages like Sólheimar, where your friends and non-biological family are merely steps away.

The neighbors and friends who frequently stop by are just as important as the skilled nursing care that residents receive. These are neighbors that they have known since they were young. For those with and without language limitations due to disabilities, it's not the words that count. It's the warmth that is felt; warmth that is just as, if not more, communicative. In fact, under these circumstances, words often get in the way as visitors struggle to come up with things to say to make somebody feel better. The warmth of easy company reminds me of two puppies lying with one's head over the neck of the other, relaxed on the couch for hours.

There are so many people who need a place like this; we all need a place like this. We've got to start creating more humane, community-based village settings like Bláskógar in the U.S. and around the world.

A staff meeting at Bláskógar.

The dining room: exuding hygge and coziness. Sensitive lighting (natural and artificial), perfect acoustics, and warm feelings abound.

CHAPTER 6

Art is the quiet connector where words sometimes fail to say all that is important and meaningful.

The Big Play: Leikfélag Sólheima (The Theatre Club) and Performing Arts

One late night at my office in Northern California, I was perusing YouTube and stumbled across a video of Sólheimar's annual play production. I watched part of it in fascination. I walked home in the middle of the night and restrained myself until 7:00 am when I woke my daughter up: "Jessie, get up a little early this morning. I've got to show you a video before school." Reluctantly and sleepily, the 15-year-old obliged while I happily rewatched it for the second time. I couldn't believe how well it was done, considering the fact that there were only a couple of professional actors involved. Most of the cast had autism or Down syndrome—only a few were neurotypical. My daughter was as enthusiastic as I was—which is rare—so I knew I was on to something. Though the play isn't exactly a professional production, it is clear that those involved are tapping into their creativity, having fun, and pursuing their potential. These people often have difficulty with life's basic tasks, but they step up to play an instrumental role in this extraordinary production. And as a result, their self-worth is affirmed; they are accepted as they are.

DOI: 10.4324/9781003642336-7

Teamwork.

Pride and Purpose

You can see in their eyes that the actors are motivated to knock it out of the park—their hearts are clearly in it. Several social workers attested that "for months afterward, they are walking on air." Remembering all their lines and maintaining attention and focus for almost two hours is a huge challenge—but when the play is over, the actors always receive a standing ovation. Memorizing the lines facilitates ease with language that allows for more expressive conversation—a way of communicating that can be very difficult to achieve, sometimes impossible, for those with autism or Down syndrome. It encourages communication that works for both people with and without neurodiversity. The confidence, the smiles, the teamwork—this play instills a sense of purpose: "I not only fit in, but I feel famous for a period of time! I am somebody. In fact, I'm special."

People with Down syndrome and autism come out of their shells in unique ways in a play.

Art as Critical

It is argued that art is integral to achieving a full life. There are many forms of art that can be pursued to give meaning to our lives: singing in a choir, playing an instrument, drawing, writing, or painting. Certainly, being in a major play or musical fosters joy. "I was in the play," says one of the 80-year-old residents, six months after the production. It sticks with them. It's meaningful and powerful to do something that they can be extremely proud of.

Sometimes, the musical includes unique dances where individuals take turns choreographing the dance during rehearsal. Many of the residents are involved behind the scenes of the play; it is a great place to encourage and develop leadership skills.

Personal Growth

I would argue that Sólheimar's yearly play does as much to foster growth, self-confidence, and a sense of inclusion as any of life's other activities. The gratification is deep.

Community is what this book is all about: the nexus between community and quality of life is imperative for everyone, especially for those with autism or Down syndrome. The Sólheimar play is all about inclusion and, therefore, community.

Prior to living at Sólheimar, these adults previously spent way too much time alone, whether in their rooms at home or in an institution. Staying in your room does not allow you to reach your potential; it is not the way to live life optimally. Being included and needed and participating in activities such as the Sólheimar play helps these folks to live their lives optimally. It requires real teamwork and deep commitment, and it connects people to their community; they don't fly off to their next gig the following day as they would in a professional play. They see each other again tomorrow at lunch, in a workshop, or at work. They depend on each other to play their parts at work again tomorrow.

> *Tomorrow I will go to work, practice my other skills, or solve a shared house problem with others . . . but for right now, I'll listen carefully and try to understand what my fellow actor is expressing. I'll give him or her the benefit of the doubt, because we did it together.*

Bring them to rehearsal, then forward to stage front. Give them a voice in the story.

Interview with an Actor

(The following is an interview with a resident involved in the theater productions.)

Socially, how did you feel before you started in the theater program?

I felt well!

What made you want to join the theater group?

I wanted to be famous!

How did you feel during the role selection process, where they were selecting different people to play different characters?

Well, I wanted a big role!

Who ends up deciding who gets each role?

The director and I decided together. But I knew what role I wanted to play before that.

What Role Did You End Up Playing?

Last year I got to play the Othum in the theater play "Looking for the Summer."

The year before that, I was in "Puss In Boots." I was also in the classic fairytale "The Three Little Pigs."

What was it like learning the role, and how were you encouraged and inspired by your peers?

It was great, I wanted a longer text, and I learned it in one or two weeks. Some of the other actors needed six weeks.

How did you feel before the show started?

A combination of excited and nervous.

How did you feel during the play when you were on stage in front of everyone?

I felt like I could conquer the world!

How did you feel a day after the theater show?

I think about what will happen during the next show and the fun I will have.

How did you feel working in a group?

Well!

How did you feel working with people with and without disabilities?

Well!

How do the audience and the guests feel when they're watching a play where some of the actors have disabilities?

I think that people feel good seeing me involved in a play. And my mother is my number one fan!

Performers enjoy rehearsals because they help to get them in the mood and engender confidence.

Singing and Dancing—Other Performing Arts at Sólheimar

Free-form modern dance allows for expression and exploration; it can be choreographed with or without partners. Yoga, dance, and movement-based practices are popular activities in the evenings at Sólheimar.

National Attention

Almost everyone in Iceland is familiar with Sólheimar, partially because the play was performed around the island five times last year—all to entirely sold-out audiences, including at the Icelandic National Theater in Reykjavik, Iceland's capital city. It is performed across the country every year, sometimes to people whom later make significant financial contributions to the Sólheimar community.

The play, as well as resident Reynir Pétur's solo circumnavigation of Iceland (a camera crew followed him for the entire expedition), have both brought attention to Sólheimar recently. Both Reynir's expedition and the play emphasize the fact that these folks have many unique capabilities that are too often overlooked and lost: they are a positive example of "One Life, Live It!"

Sólheimar Makes Everyone in Iceland Proud

On my first book tour in Iceland (for a previous book, *Cohousing Communities*) and through my various talks (Iceland Architecture Association, the School of Architecture at the University of Iceland, and others), I've learned that many people in Iceland have visited Sólheimar and have great admiration for what they do there. But, witnessing the connection between community and quality of life is still too rare, even in Iceland. Community is elusive—if not nebulous—and it's difficult to assign

A recital on the day celebrating Römpum upp Ísland (Ramp Up Iceland), the inauguration of accessibility ramp installation in Sólheimar and all across Iceland in 2023.

The choir practices a lot and performs frequently. It's a common occurrence at gatherings.

Reynir Pétur Steinunnarson (red jacket) was awarded the badge of honor of the Icelandic Falcon Order for achievements and progress for the benefit of the disabled—a well-deserved honor that those at Sólheimar are very proud of.

a dollar value to it. Community is indeed priceless, but there is only one ecovillage like Sólheimar in Iceland. There is a dire need to create more of these villages; the desire to do so is increasing in popularity as the benefits of these communities are becoming widely recognized internationally. See Chapters 9 and 10.

Garnering Support in Iceland

Sólheimar is well recognized as a model. It seems that everyone wants to support the success of this community, even if it's just by purchasing a ticket to the play and embracing an opportunity to see others' support and be seen as a supporter. Sólheimar's branding is successful. They have tapped into heartfelt public sentiments like, "This is the way it should be," "It *is* doable," "Imagine all the people," and more. If you know about Sólheimar, you want to support it.

Characters, for sure.

Staff and Volunteers Are Key to a Successful Production

More than anything else, it takes an infrastructure of staff and volunteers for the big play's success over the years—in other words, it takes a community. Over half of the residents participate in the show's production. Volunteers—such as the director Guðmundur Lúðvík Þorvaldsson, who has written and directed the show numerous times—also play a vital role.

Halli Valli, Head Developmental Therapist, not only runs the woodworking studio and takes on other leadership roles at Sólheimar but also helps with directing, writing music, and acting in the play! You can clearly see the love he has for his work and for the residents there: what a special place it is to be cared for by people like Halli Valli. Hats off to him!

No One Is Invisible

Often, in our society, people with disabilities can be quiet, hidden, or seemingly invisible. It's painful to see anyone being mistreated or ignored; after all, they are all human. *One Life, Live It* calls for enhancing the quality of life for all people; Sesselja got this right from the beginning.

Sesselja as Grassroots Organizer

Sesselja understood networking and how to garner her resources to ensure that the residents were not only comfortable and safe but also could pursue purposeful, meaningful lives. These days, you can get an undergraduate or graduate degree in communications; they have made the science of broadcasting, framing, and branding a message. We empirically know how to do this. Exposure is needed so that the folks who want to support Sólheimar are also not invisible. No one is invisible—everyone who helps make it possible is known and appreciated. In the next chapter, we'll examine the staff that keep Sólheimar running.

The director Guðmundur setting the players up for success.
Photo by Ljósmyndir Leifur Þór Ragnarsson.

The play is an appreciated cultural movement, both inside and outside of the community. It has numerous components: script writing, music writing, back-of-house operations, front-of-house operations, promotional work, lighting, stage design, costumes, venue operations, the list goes on. Producing the show is not a small task, but it is a worthwhile, purpose-driven, and community-building one.

In the U.S., we give the billionaires and millionaires tax breaks. Some say it's in Icelanders' nature to care about their most vulnerable people, but Iceland hasn't always been so community-focused. It took a multitude of grassroots organizers like Sesselja to get them there. As George Lakey says in his book *Viking Economics*, no one person really makes a difference in consequence, but if enough people work at it, a cumulation of small differences will have an enormous impact.

CHAPTER 7

Kindness is a way of life here—fostering friendship in a community built on care and respect.

Staff (Friends) of Sólheimar

Sólheimar's staff is truly devoted. The ecovillage is brimming with service-minded people; it warms your heart to watch them interact with the residents. Residents with disabilities are not called "patients," and everyone is referred to as friends.

Respect and Care: An Introduction to the Staff at Sólheimar

In my interview with Dagný Davíðsdóttir, Head Developmental Coach at Sólheimar, she described how residents are supported and how their independence is fostered. Staff are willing to follow residents' curiosities and try different things; they take the time to listen. Respect and care are baked into the Sólheimar culture. The pedagogical approach called gentle teaching is widely practiced there. My observation is that gentle teaching is a skill that some people are more predisposed to than others—they intuitively strive to perfect it. These are the kinds of people who work and want to work at Sólheimar.

DOI: 10.4324/9781003642336-8

The staff at Sólheimar includes sociologists, accountants, tutors, janitors, chefs, educators, counselors, gardeners, therapists, and more.

Dagný described Sólheimar as a wonderful place to work; the staff willingly helps each other out and is especially supportive of new hires. Workers are an essential part of Sólheimar, and together with the villagers they all compose the community. "Everyone feels that we all have to have a purpose in life." They set each other up for success.

We asked Margarita, a former project manager at Sólheimar, "How has your life changed since working in Sólheimar? Have you made sacrifices?" She responded by saying,

> *Working and living in Sólheimar is not just a job or just moving to a new place. It is a change of lifestyle. I have to say that there are no sacrifices; you actually gain so much from living there. You get to throw away your bad habits, such as going to unnecessary places like shopping malls, and consuming too much food, gasoline, and energy. You become social instead of isolating yourself inside your little apartment in the city. You actually get to know your neighbor, care for your neighbor. It is rewarding both mentally and physically.*

The official job of the staff is to support individuals, determining:

1. *What does this person need?*
2. *What service can we provide?*
3. *What do they want?*
4. *How will we provide it?*

These are the fundamentals—but it's about more than that. What I observed at Sólheimar was profound. If someone was grieving, they would get special support; someone would grieve with them. If someone was depressed, another person would keep them company, even if they were on the clock. They met each other where they were—emotionally and physically. If a resident was stuck on the couch, a staff member (or another resident) sat in a chair across from them; they were there for them. Finding something that folks are really motivated to do and are really interested in gives them a sense of purpose. Getting everyone involved and connected takes extraordinary skill and dedication.

Gentle Teaching: A Compassionate Approach to Human Connection

The person-centered approach of gentle teaching aims to enhance the overall quality of life for individuals. Gentle teaching is grounded in a deep understanding that every individual, regardless of personal abilities or challenges, has the capacity for positive change and connection with one another. By addressing not only basic needs but also emotional and social needs, individuals experience a more fulfilling and meaningful life within their communities. Gentle teaching encourages social interaction and the development of interpersonal skills. Through positive relationships with caregivers and peers, individuals learn and practice social skills, contributing to their ability to connect with others and participate in community life.

See box at the end of the chapter for a detailed explanation of Gentle Teaching.

The staff at Sólheimar treat everyone with respect and kindness; a genuine love for their community is evident.

This is a place where joy is; it is where the heart is. If you partake in heart-warming activities, then you feel contented over and over again.

Meeting a Few of the Staff Members

Sólheimar has about 100 residents: about 45 have autism or Down syndrome. There are around a dozen social workers (or "social educators," as they say), six staff members who lead art workshops, ten who lead "practical" endeavors such as maintenance, greenhouses, cooking, and the like. There are approximately eight staff members involved in accounting and administration, ten volunteers and around two dozen resident spouses and children.

Sólheimar attracts amazing staff members like Halli Valli and many others.

A volunteer through Worldwide Friends.

Sólheimar is driven by its emphasis on love and support for every person in the community; this attracts many amazing staff members like Halli Valli. Halli Valli is a skilled, inspired, and highly motivated social worker. He organizes the woodworking shop and musical events—all integral aspects of the communal village.

Piotr, from Poland, worked in Sólheimar for almost three years managing the Sunna Horticultural Center and Greenhouses (the current manager is a very capable woman named 'Ina). Piotr works with volunteers from around the world who are curious about how Sólheimar works; they are inspired to take lessons learned from Sólheimar back to their home countries. Volunteers are easier to come by when the public is aware of all that Sólheimar has to offer.

The real question is whether any of these volunteers will bring the knowledge back to where they came from. To make meaningful change, you need a big vision, a team of talented people, and a plan. Every project like this needs at least one inspired person who brings the definitive vision to the table. Then they can assemble a team and a comprehensive plan. See Chapter 10.

The behind-the-scenes work is critical to keeping the organization running smoothly.

Many social workers impressed me as they had a very easy and loving manner with friends at Sólheimar—friends, not clients. The lack of hierarchy is critical; everyone is a peer, and there is no subordination. Most residents are adults and want as much respect as any other adult anywhere else. Social workers like the ones pictured on these pages continually demonstrate respect: hourly, weekly, monthly, and yearly. Love and equality are exuded and taught—this is often referred to as gentle teaching, and it is a big part of Sólheimar's culture.

Horsing around, wrestling, and playing after dinner in one of the shared houses.

Piotr, seen here working at Sunna HQ.

This social worker impressed me with a very easy, loving manner with friends and residents who lived there.

A Philosophy of Friends

The staff of Sólheimar embraces a philosophy of friends; they do not view residents as "clients" or "patients":

> *I will give them my attention like I would any other friend—hanging on their every word and expression and being jovial when they're down and in need. I'm not their boss, not even their guide—I am their peer, their equal. Whatever the issue is, we will solve it together. I will not lecture; I will not judge. I'm your friend, and whatever it is, we will discuss it and solve it together.*

You are, he is, she is, my dear friend. I will give you attention like I would any other friend.

Interview with Lisa Saga, Volunteer at Sólheimar

Interviewer: Rory Kuczek

Lisa is a volunteer/staff member at Sólheimar residing with her husband, Guillaume. She works in the village's greenhouse and art workshops. Lisa had been at Sólheimar for about six months at the time of this interview.

Why have you chosen to live in cohousing and this particular ecovillage?

We left our previous volunteer job (it did not suit us) and drove around Iceland . . . It was a Sunday; one of those days of dreadful Scandinavian weather, heavy skies full of rain falling constantly, and everything was colored grey. All the places we checked didn't look promising, and we were close to losing hope and probably even leaving the country. I suddenly remembered that years ago, I had heard of a small ecovillage located somewhere in the region we were passing by. We quickly found the route and drove there—simply following our intuition and not knowing much about the place. It was rainy, and the whole village looked very quiet as we arrived.

For a while, we couldn't find anyone to talk to until suddenly, there was a woman walking towards us. As we quickly introduced ourselves and explained our visit, she told us that she was a manager, and just this morning, she woke up thinking about where on earth she could find two new interns that the village needed. What was most peculiar was that they were especially looking for someone eager to help at their fantastic greenhouses but who was also focused on art. I have a background as an illustrator and am passionate about several forms of art—as much about bees as growing sprouts. In addition to that, they were looking for someone with technical and musical skills-both of which excite my husband. You can imagine the decision was mutual and made promptly; we moved in the day after! As we signed our contracts as volunteers, we were provided with a room in a house shared by a few people, which we gladly accepted because both of us had experience living in a similar place previously. To make a long story short, it feels more like the place called us out of nowhere and chose us to come and stay.

How has life changed for you? Did you have to sacrifice anything?

I tend to believe that our lives have changed towards even more peace and acceptance, filling both me and my husband since we've moved here. Living in nature and working with it, as well as working with home people and art (after a couple of months, I moved to the art workshop, and Guillaume is now mainly working at the local theatre), feels like a dream coming true. We learn daily from everything and everyone that surrounds and touches us.

We still have a chance to help with the growing greens and the dark soil from time to time, so it is a perfect combination of what we love and what we want to do in this life. And of course, this provides inner peace, confidence, and joy.

What are some things that would benefit the residents?

Regarding new options of benefits for residents, I would name more possibilities for traveling and experiencing the land and the surrounding areas. Other activities related to art, especially exhibiting and curating their work not only within but also outside of Sólheimar, as well as having a bigger focus on psychological and physiological hygiene and sex education for younger generations living and growing in the village.

How do you think you influence Sólheimar as an individual?

Sólheimar makes me look at the life happening around me with more brightness and smiles. It teaches me to be sincere and grateful for small and big blessings and, most importantly, it guides me toward an attitude of acceptance. I also feel and celebrate my professional growth that is taking place here and now.

Gentle Teaching: A Compassionate Approach to Human Connection

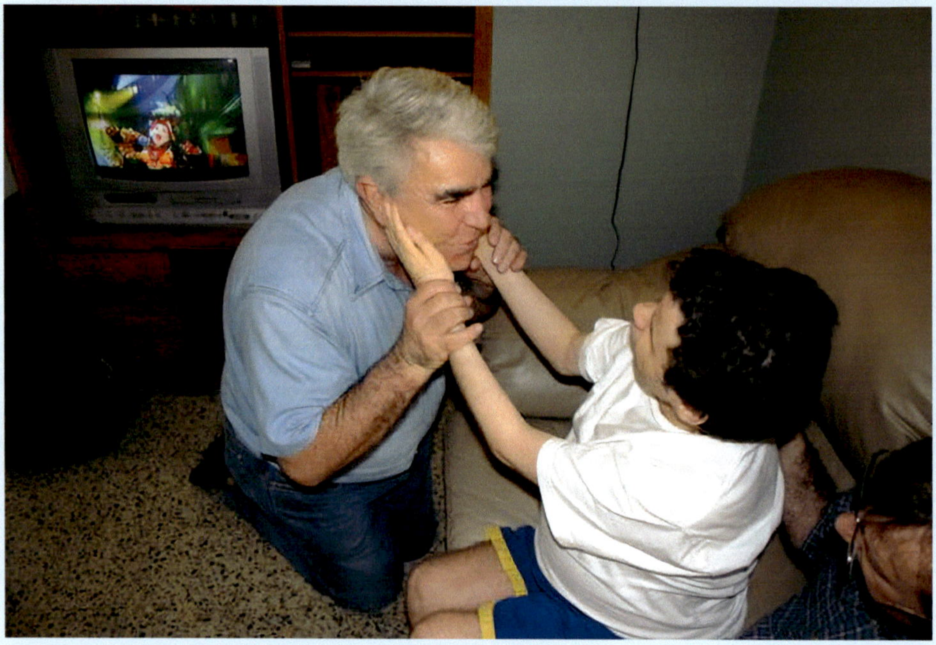

This section is inspired by the formal work, practices, and teachings of John McGee, PhD, author, and teacher. It is also inspired by my own observations of Sólheimar and from designing and living in cohousing communities for the last 40 years. It was written with the help of my friend Cam Dore, an experienced Gentle Teaching practitioner. It is clear that Sólheimar practices their own version of Gentle Teaching based on their own experiences. This Gentle Teaching practice has evolved at Sólheimar since 1930, and they implement it as well as I have seen anywhere. Gentle Teaching has evolved since animals have nurtured their young and have adapted as we strive to build a civilized society. While we have a long way to go to employ it widely as a species, Sólheimar appears to practice Gentle Teaching every day.

In the realm of caregiving and support for marginalized individuals living with developmental disabilities, Gentle Teaching stands out as a philosophy that prioritizes connection, empathy, and compassion. It seeks to create environments that foster growth, interdependence, and a sense of well-being for individuals with diverse needs. Worldwide, communities strive to practice Gentle Teaching; many have gravitated to it naturally because it best facilitates their goals.

The Pedagogy of Gentle Teaching

At its core, Gentle Teaching is not merely a set of techniques or strategies; it is a philosophy that permeates every aspect of caregiving and support. Gentle Teaching is grounded in a deep understanding of human nature and the belief that every individual, regardless of their abilities or challenges, has the capacity for positive change and connection with one another.

Gentle Teaching is about unconditional love. It recognizes that many people are burdened with memories of distrust and fear, that their hearts are broken, and that a simple lack of inclusion or acceptance is a legitimate cause. It focuses on teaching them a sense of companionship. Through this process, violent behaviors begin to disappear, and new ones emerge. Gentle Teaching incorporates compassion as an alternative to the reactive and restrictive practices that are commonplace in working with those who have complex needs. The central purpose is to nurture, teach, and sustain a sense of companionship, connectedness, and community for those who have repeatedly experienced an existence of disconnectedness, isolation, and loneliness.

The principles of Gentle Teaching are based on the premise that all individuals have a right to feel safe and valued: in their homes; with their families and caregivers; in their neighborhood and physical community; and at their jobs, schools, or other places where daily activities occur. Those who are most vulnerable require daily predictability and structure. They also need to interactively engage with others who are positive and uplifting (vs. critical and demanding). This is truly a cultural shift to—or, in some cases, a deepening of—those principles that provide a solid base for helping individuals experience companionship and connectedness. It serves as a foundation for other models of treatment and teaching that are specific to the needs of the individual.

By nurturing a culture of acceptance, gentleness, and empathy with Gentle Teaching, we can foster a psychology of interdependence, where every human being can live connected with others in equal and mutual relationships embedded in loving and caring communities. These communities invite individuals to develop healthy qualities for their own benefit and others. The ideal companionship has four main parts:

1. ***Feeling safe at all times***

   Feeling safe is the foundation for building trusting, meaningful relationships. This includes feeling emotionally, physically, psychologically, and environmentally safe.

2. ***Feeling loved by each other***

   Our goal is to create cultures of support where everyone feels valued, regardless of their interactional challenges. Recognizing that behaviors are a symptom of emotional discomfort, a person does not need to earn approval. It is essential to support a person so that they can experience the unconditional love they deserve.

3. ***Feeling loving towards each other***

   To truly be a part of a community, one must find value in kinship with others. It is a caregiver's responsibility to demonstrate the skills necessary to become connected to the people around us and to assist others in nurturing meaningful relationships.

4. ***Engaging and feeling connected with each other***

   Discovering ways to get involved in meaningful activities, finding value in relationships, and building connections within the community are essential aspects of one's life journey. Michael Vincent, a long-time Gentle Teaching trainer, sums it up by saying, "The central purpose of our presence in the lives of others is to nurture, teach, and sustain the experience of connectedness, companionship, and community." In my observation, this is the foundation of "One Life, Live It!" and of Sólheimar's existence.

Via GentleTeaching.com and Gentle Teaching International "Defining Gentle Teaching" (2018)

The Four Tools

By using the following four tools, educators and caregivers are taught that they themselves can be instruments of peace by communicating non-violence, forgiveness, empathy, and total acceptance. These tools are not fancy, tricky to use, or expensive. They are things that we use every day to connect with those around us—our hands, our eyes, our words, and our presence. These tools are instruments to connect and build relationships with those around us.

1. Our Hands

Touch is an instrument that involves carefully offered embraces, pats on the back, or arms around the shoulder. Not all people want to be touched. Sometimes, it may be too traumatizing and can produce fearful flashbacks for survivors of physical or sexual abuse. Context is key.

The practice of touch varies from culture to culture. In cultures that focus on the individual, touch is often regarded as inappropriate and unprofessional. In other cultures, it is a strong expression of human connectedness and solidarity. Even in individualistic cultures, touch is still considered to be a positive expression of love toward children and the elderly.

Many professionals and administrators are afraid of any touch in educational or caregiving settings unless it is for the purpose of physical management. They express deep concerns, such as: "How will an individual learn boundaries?" Gentle Teaching's use of touch, such as a hug, is intentionally platonic and not sexual in any way. That said, educators and caregivers need to proceed with great care in the use of touch, ensuring that these acts are seen as symbols of companionship and community. Many people think that Gentle Teaching is all about hugs. Physical contact is an important aspect of the approach because it can be a very concrete expression of the feeling "I am safe with you. And you are safe with me." Touch is employed as a ritual in a culture of gentleness; it becomes a symbol of what this culture is all about—namely, companionship and connectedness. "I could sure use a hug!" or "Do you want a hug?" are acceptable in this setting. The use of loving touch gradually takes on a meaning of gentle, compassionate understanding. The caregiver's hands can be concrete expressions that enable an environment of love and safety.

2. Our Eyes

Educators and caregivers can utilize their gaze as a strong tool, allowing them to look into murky and shattered hearts to bring warmth, consolation, and healing. Eye contact can be like tender hands or pounding fists. One must be deeply present in the moment and understand that even one's gaze sends a strong message.

3. Our Words

Perhaps the most powerful tool in a culture of gentleness is our words. Our words are not simply "words" when they are interpreted alongside the softness in our faces, the tone and rhythm of our voices, the twinkle in our eyes, the reaching out of our arms, and the way we look at those around us. Our words must be uplifting and warm; each syllable that we emit should be loaded with honor, kindness, and love. We must understand the power of our words, their sounds, and their rhythm. In a culture of gentleness, words are not used to degrade, reprimand, blame, or sermonize. They are used to honor, console, and uplift. The tool that is used (or misused) all too often is our words. Educators and caregivers often mistakenly think that their primary role is to teach each person to behave by threatening bad behavior, issuing blame, and scolding ("You know better!"). Teachers and caregivers too often emphasize dull behavioral reinforcements, such as, "Good job" or "No, stop that!" These expressions are not beneficial for self-esteem or creating caring relationships. Rather, our words should signal feelings of safety and love. Educators and caregivers need to recognize that all of their interactions add up and progressively contribute to a long-term dialogue that influences the establishment of self-esteem in all of their relationships/kinships. A large part of this dialogue simply involves listening, reading between the lines, understanding each person's life story, and interpreting feelings that underlie actions.

4. Our Presence

Gentle Teaching is concerned with the intentionality of one's presence in each moment. The messages that a teacher or caregiver (and, in the case of a cohousing community, a neighbor) sends—in moments of struggle or joy—are consequential. "Behavioral change" is only a secondary goal; the teacher or caregiver must be authentic in finding ways to express love and understanding in the moment. It is critical to be aware that one's mere presence communicates a thousand words.

Impact on Individuals

By fostering a culture of acceptance, tenderness, and empathy, Gentle Teaching increases self-esteem and a sense of self-worth. The emphasis on positive reinforcement (rewarding of a "desirable" behavior) in Gentle Teaching often leads to a reduction in challenging behaviors. By addressing the root causes of behaviors and providing alternative, positive outlets, caregivers can create an environment where individuals feel understood and supported.

Finally, Gentle Teaching represents a paradigm shift in the care and support of marginalized individuals and those with developmental disabilities. By focusing on unconditional acceptance, kindness, and empathy, Gentle Teaching goes beyond traditional approaches to create environments that nurture growth, connection, and a sense of well-being.

The essence of Gentle Teaching is the container—the vessel—for the life-changing concepts presented in this book. Gentle Teaching necessitates a proximate community. In most of the world, symptoms are treated only when one is at the therapist, the doctor, or at home. When someone is treated with Gentle Teaching and subsequently sent back home, to the shared house, or to the shelter, it doesn't work. When the environment is set up like Sólheimar, like a proximate village in which everyone practices the compassion of Gentle Teaching in all their environments—it *can* work. Every organization can develop its own method, but first and foremost, it must start with a clear and resolved intention.

CHAPTER 8

There is so much in life that we can only do in common with others. That is especially true in the realm of economics. Economics can effectively help stitch us together.

The Economics and Management of Sólheimar

By far, the most consequential economic practice that sets Sólheimar apart is an embodiment of the gift economy. The gifts of time, attention, consideration, recognition, skill sharing, help, appreciation, and love are all of great value in Sólheimar's economy. The help required—most of it coming from peers—to figure out the whole life deal; the ride to the grocery store when there is too much to carry on the bus; the assistance given when a neighbor needs your personal skills to, say, repair their bike chain; this paperwork, or that paperwork—it is all done alongside and with the help of others. "How come I can't find something on my phone?" The simplest solution is to ask someone nearby who knows and understands you. "My mom hasn't called in a week; I'm worried about my brother's failing health . . ." the perils of life are shared by those around you. Supporting each other through proximal, foundational, and therapeutic relationships is not only less costly for governments and families but can be more valuable and authentic when accomplished through meaningful and trusting friendships.

DOI: 10.4324/9781003642336-9

Governments often have a hard time determining ideal economic systems for the people they govern. More importantly, however, they tend to get the social math wrong. For example, sometimes a government will transition from four people in a shared house to six—attempting to make it more "economical"—only to find that it doesn't work socially. This results in a fundamentally less economical structure.

The help and the time is given to one another, the outpouring of emotions for each other, the affection and respect that moves people towards each other—these all hold significant value at Sólheimar.

Value-adding and keeping costs down.

Everything shifts in a community-first approach. Four rooms work great when you're part of a community—there are plenty of social opportunities right outside your door.

The making of useful things—for example, repurposing scraps of wood to make instruments, canning fruits and vegetables from the garden, etc.—requires teamwork and produces gratification, purpose, and satisfaction. In a culture of sustainability, emphasis is placed on reusing, repurposing, and adding value by transforming raw and recycled materials into art and gifts. Sólheimar residents and staff prioritize well-being and accomplish a lifestyle beyond what is possible with government subsidies alone.

Sólheimar makes a great deal of "products" from what they grow and create there. It helps sustain them economically.

Sacred Economics

An essay based on the book Sacred Economics: Money, Gift, and Society in the Age of Transition *by Charles Eisenstein and our impression of the key social economics at Sólheimar.*

In the modern economy, goods and services are based on extraction, mass production, and commercialization. "Wealth" is created by taking something that was once free or inexpensive and selling it for more than you spent acquiring it. Contrast this commodification-based system with a community-based system where you know and need each other, and your energy is spent on building and sustaining interdependent and enriching relationships. That deep longing for connection and substance inherent in all of us can be satisfied. Interdependent relationships contain what Charles Eisenstein calls "Sacred Economics," as described in his eponymous book.

"Please help me look for something," "Please show me how to make bread:" the gift economy is infinite. No physical object is better than the relationships that blossom into life-long friendships. Accomplishing day-to-day tasks together and in close proximity to one another allows these bonds to form organically. The economy of meaningful life is the currency of consequence and was invented before money. The demise of the gift economy has led to social alienation, competition, and the need for continuous growth. But the world can't sustain limitless, linear growth. Instead, we need to focus less on convenience and independence and more on truly sustainable currencies that fulfill the soul and nourish the planet and each other.

When a close friend or loved one dies, you can heal and learn how to be whole again. There is nothing like being surrounded by others who help you face life's challenges head-on and discover your self-worth. We can mitigate all the emotional compromises that contemporary life necessitates, *together*.

Most people with autism feel a sense of injustice; they don't have the perceived benefits that others have. It takes a village to feel like you have everything you need and deserve: loving brothers and sisters, joy, music, direction, and the rest. A sense of purpose without the unending, unsettling need for more—without greed—can be achieved through sacred economics.

Cost to Parents and Families

A parent planning a new cohousing community once told me that he and his wife went on a trip for their 30th anniversary and had to take their 24-year-old autistic son with them. Having to book two hotel rooms, pay for extra meals, and take care of their son during their celebratory trip was not economically or emotionally ideal. Paying for a grown child who is fully dependent on you is exorbitantly expensive—$20–40k per year—and there are rarely better alternative options. Parents of special needs children often find themselves staring down a six-figure bill to cover the cost of lifetime care. Under the circumstances that

Excerpt From Chapter 22: "Community and the Unquantifiable" in Sacred Economics, by Charles Eisenstein

Earlier in this book, I described the disconnection and loneliness of a society in which nearly all social capital, nearly all relationships, have been converted to paid services, in which distant strangers meet nearly all of our material needs, in which we can always "pay someone else to do it"; in which the unspoken knowledge *I don't need you* pervades our social gatherings, rendering them vacuous and dispensable. Such is the pinnacle of civilization, the end point of centuries of increasing affluence: lonely people in boxes, living in a world of strangers, dependent on money, enslaved to debt—and incinerating the planet's natural and social capital to stay that way. We have no community because community is woven from gifts. How can we create a community when we pay for all we need?

Community is not some add-on to our other needs, not a separate ingredient for happiness, along with food, shelter, music, touch, intellectual stimulation, and other forms of physical and spiritual nourishment. Community arises from meeting these needs. There is no community possible among a group of people who do not need each other. Therefore, any life that seeks to be independent of other people to meet of one's needs is a life without community.

...

The situation in America, the most highly monetized society the world has ever known, is this: some of our needs are vastly overfulfilled while others go tragically unmet. We in the richest societies have too many calories even as we starve for beautiful, fresh food; we have overlarge houses but lack spaces that truly embody our individuality and connectedness; media surround us everywhere while we starve for authentic communication. We are offered entertainment every second of the day but lack the chance to play. In the ubiquitous realm of money, we hunger for all that is intimate, personal, and unique.

...

Clearly, the transition to a sacred economy accompanies a transition in our psychology. Community, which in today's parlance usually means proximity or a mere network, is a much deeper kind of connection than that: it is a sharing of one's being, an expansion of oneself. To be in a community is to be in a personal, interdependent relationship, and it comes with a price: our illusion of independence, our freedom from obligation. You can't have it both ways. If you want community, you must be willing to be obligated, dependent, tied, and attached. You will give and receive gifts that you cannot just buy somewhere. You will not be able to easily find another source. You *need* each other.

...

We are starving for spiritual nourishment. We are starving for a life that is personal, connected, and meaningful. By choice, that is where we will direct our energy. When we do so, the community will arise anew because this spiritual nourishment can only come to us as a gift, as part of a web of gifts in which we participate as a giver and a receiver.

the family can't afford to provide this care, their child may become homeless or displaced to the "next empty bed" of a group home or adult foster care. In California, this costs about $75k per patient annually and is covered by taxpayers. These extra costs are best mitigated by a community setting instead.

The cost of doing nothing, as articulated by activist Desiree Kameka Galloway, is enormous.

> *This population will almost always outlive their parents—if they didn't have the means and skills to do appropriate estate planning and take out a big life insurance policy that dumps into a Special Needs Trust—the cost goes back to the taxpayers at an enormous annual Medicaid bill . . . helping families invest in housing in cooperative and compassionate cohousing prevents the trauma of displacement, is life-changing to adults with A/I/DD, but would save our country billions—no exaggeration.*

Cost of Aging

The homeless population isn't the only thing that counties misdirect funds toward. The growing senior population in the U.S.—a significant portion of which is, in fact, homeless—is also struggling to make ends meet and often requires financial assistance. Help is provided in the form of direct subsidies from the city, county, or state itself or through the efforts of non-profits who are also often subsidized (by donors, etc.).

It's expensive to grow old in the U.S. for both the seniors and the institutions that provide for them. Look at San Diego, which is one of the country's highest cost-of-living cities. According to the Elder Index, a tool that the California state government uses to calculate senior living expenses, it costs a senior in good health living only on their savings and social security nearly $28,000 to accommodate their needs. And this is only when they're not paying rent. If they're a renter, it costs at least $37,000. If they still have a mortgage, it costs more than $47,000. That's a higher cost of living than for a working non-senior. To alleviate the burden—especially for seniors in poverty, in poor health, or both—non-profits like Serving Seniors donate significant chunks of time and money to senior care. Last year, they spent $8 million to distribute 1.2 million meals to elderly folks who experienced food insecurity. They spent another $2.5 million on health checks and social services—services provided to check on their well-being and remove them from isolation. These costs double for seniors with I/DD.

Sacramento, California, and its surrounding counties spent $9.7 million on nutritional services, delivering over 700,000 meals to nearly 5,400 seniors annually. This is not fiscally or environmentally sustainable, and it doesn't include the hidden costs that come from the fire and police departments. Calls for assistance to the fire department are becoming so frequent that cities are beginning to charge fees if it turns out the call is not an emergency.

It is commonplace for one person (often a family member) to devote their lives to taking care of a neurodiverse family member. Not only does it cost these individuals their autonomy, but the economic

The box on homelessness (on page 137) is for economic comparison. The most economical solution for homelessness and many other situations that are subsidized by governments (taxpayers) is to get people set up in a cooperative community. Governments can be more successful if they do not waste massive amounts of money by virtue of neglect.

costs to society are exorbitant as skilled workers are lost when relatives must fill in as full-time caregivers.

In a community, especially one where additional care may be necessary for seniors with autism or Down syndrome, these costs are mitigated. It's unnecessary for meals to be delivered, as the community can help provide them. It's unnecessary to provide wellness and social checks because friends and neighbors are always there to provide company. Certainly, calls to the fire department are reduced significantly. Millions of dollars spent on senior and neurodivergent care could be saved by actualizing genuine community.

SOURCES OF FUNDING

Funding for Sólheimar comes from a variety of sources. The local and national governments provide financial support, but less per person than at other similar institutions. Sólheimar applies for grants as well. Residents and staff pay for housing and food; residents with disabilities receive welfare assistance that they can use for rent. They sell produce from the greenhouses and the goods they create in workshops, and they rent out common spaces as venues for conferences and concerts. They even have a carbon "cap and trade" program with the forestry department. Residents earn income from working in the

This bar graph roughly outlines the different sources of income at Sólheimar.

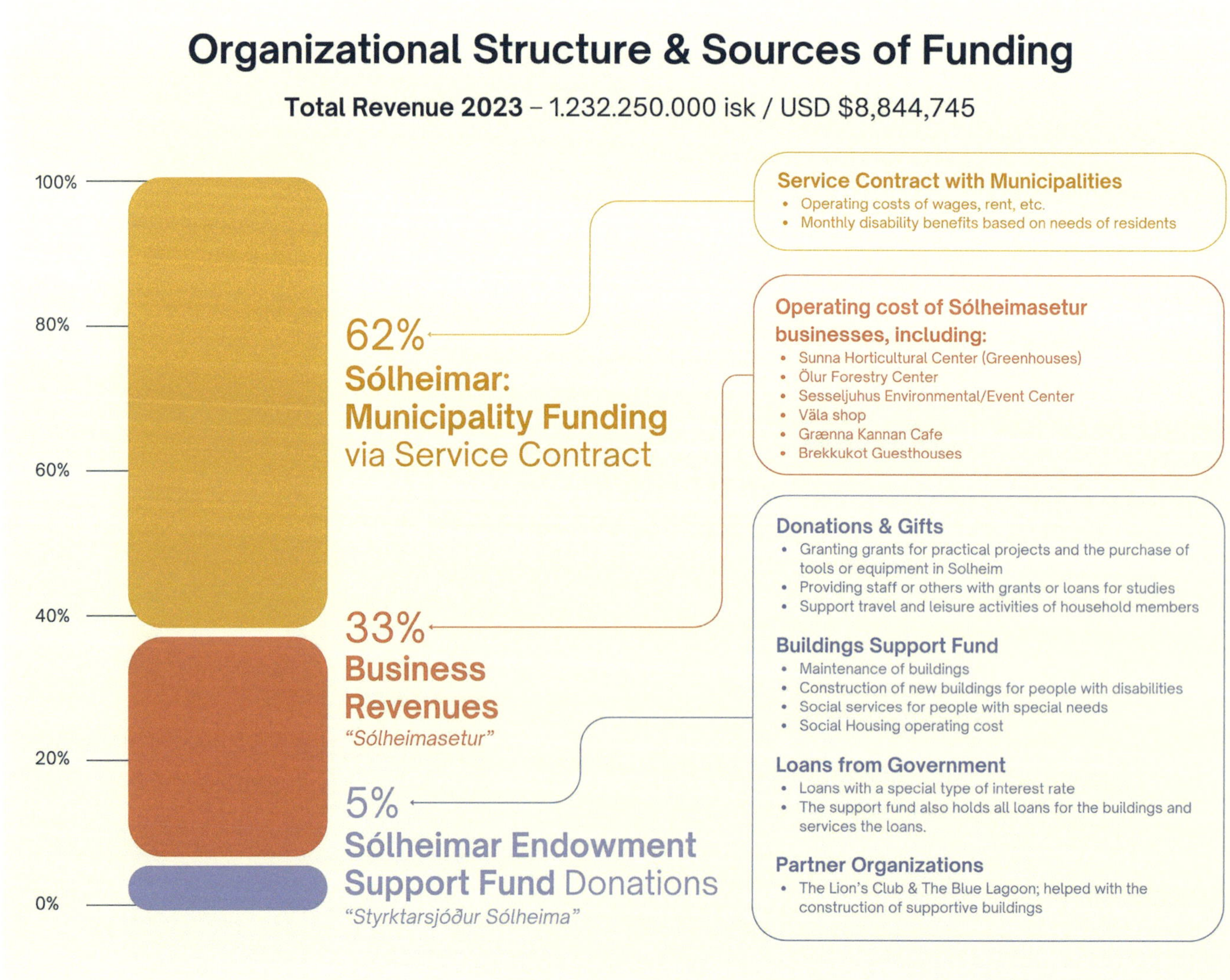

The Real Cost of Not Investing in People

Homelessness in America is just one example relevant here because the costs of homelessness to the taxpayer are now well understood.

The real economics that are not adequately considered in the U.S. and most other countries is the money spent where high-functioning neighborhoods *aren't* present. There have now been studies done on the cost of homelessness in over 30 American cities—it ranges from $30,000 to $50,000 per year per homeless person. People like to point out that half of those sleeping under bridges have mental disorders, almost as if to say, "Well, there's nothing we can do about that." But the cost to society is obvious; it's a travesty for these folks to be cast adrift. How does a grandmother explain to her 5-year-old granddaughter the specter of homelessness our country engenders? How does she justify our communities allowing people with disabilities to sleep on the street?

In the U.S., the top 7 of 100 government costs caused by homelessness are:

1. **Police Department:** Incessant police calls about a homeless person sleeping in someone's backyard, on their front porch, in their doorway, etc., and the corresponding cases.
2. **Fire Department (particularly first aid cases):** Over 50% of the fires started in the Sierra Nevada region in California in the last 20 years have been started by unhoused people in abandoned houses or the brush. Homelessness seems to be a main driver of the need for new fire trucks, costing fire departments millions of dollars.
3. **Hospitals:** Particularly the "51/50" rooms for someone hurting themselves or others. Many of those folks turn themselves in for three meals, a roof, and heat. The minimum stay is usually three to seven days.
4. **Jails:** An "obvious" solution to homelessness for some people—three meals, a roof, a bed, and blankets.
5. **County staff:** It's frustrating how much is spent on staff allocation for this problem; rarely does this provide enduring solutions.
6. **Non-profit** social services.
7. **Revenues** lost to businesses due to the specter of homelessness in downtowns.

Many of these costs can be avoided if the city or the county instead invested in adequate housing and functioning communities. Homeless populations need permanent places to reside, support systems to help them during hard times, and communities to make them feel that they belong and are accountable. For a more complete investigation into the costs of homelessness to society (Neurodiverse or Neurotypical), see the book *A Solution to Homelessness in Your Town.*

Folks with autism and Down syndrome can either contribute to the local and national economies (if they live in a functional community) or they can detract from the national economies (if they are homeless or drain government funds due to inadequate care). It is very cumbersome, if not impossible, for a family member to be capable of providing care that enables economic contribution from the affected person (See Chapter 3 for the critical scale necessary). As one I/DD activist, Paul Platner, founder of EnGaged Services, pointed out, "What happens to an economy when 10–15% of the people not working begin to work and love it?" The I/DD population is continuously caught up in a medical system that they understandably cannot navigate without extensive help.

cafe, bakery, store, greenhouse, and maintenance departments. They also earn commissions from the goods they sell. Because most residents are considered hard to employ, the government subsidizes their pay. The fact that Sólheimar has managed to keep its doors open for so long speaks to the tenacity and dedication of the staff and residents to keep the place alive. The staff's dedication is a currency of consequence. Embodying a high mission inspires the staff, which, in turn, builds and reinforces the vision.

Purpose, art, and co-counseling (friendships) require very little funding. When everyone gives a little, there is always enough for a community to grow. Most importantly, when the people affected are involved in the community's fundraising and planning, the outcome is more cost-effective and resonant for the ones who matter. Funding sources are highly influential on a project.

Non-Profit Structure

Three non-profit organizations operate under the banner of Sólheimi: *Sólheimar*, Business Revenues (*Sólheimasetur*), and the Support/Endowment Fund (*Styrktarsjóður Sólheima*). The following is a brief overview of what each organization is responsible for.

Sólheimar (In Contract with Municipalities)

In Iceland, the National government and its municipalities (64 districts total—similar to American counties) pay disability to folks who can't work. Sólheimar makes a service contract for services to disabled residents who live there and gets a monthly payment from the municipalities for the operating costs of wages, rent, and other costs. Sigurjón Örn Bórsson, chairman of Sólheimar's Board, said, "In the long run, the biggest cost is the care/social side, not the buildings."

Disabled residents also receive monthly disability benefits from the state: around 400,000 Króna per month (close to $3,000 USD) for food and rent, which is slightly higher than the average entry-level wage in Iceland. The payment in the U.S.—provided by Supplemental Social Security Income—is, on average, one-third lower.

400,000 ISK ($2,930 USD)/ person/month

x 12 months

4,800,000 ISK/year per person ($35,000 USD/person/ year)

4,800,000 ISK ($35,000 USD)

x 45 residents with disabilities

216,000,000 ISK total for the year that the government gives to residents to pay for food and rent ($1.6 Million USD/year for all 45 residents)

There are additional subsidies to Sólheimar for educational programs, workshops, special building programs and improvements, infrastructure improvements, and more. The government also pays for teachers' and counselors' salaries, whether they're working at Sólheimar or elsewhere in Iceland.

Business Revenues (Sólheimasetur)
These are what Sigurjón referred to as the "hardcore businesses."** These income drivers pay for the operating costs of Sólheimar.

- **Sunna Horticultural Center (Greenhouses)**
  The greenhouses are becoming profitable, but more importantly, they play a key role in giving residents a sense of purpose. They employ two full-time people in the winter and eight to ten full-time people in the summer.
- **Ölur Forestry Center**
  The forestry center planted 90,000 tree seedlings when it was re-established in 2019. Since then, they've scaled up quite successfully and currently deliver around 340,000 seedlings per year.

  They sell adolescent trees to nurseries, over 60 non-profits, and Icelandic jurisdictions for wind breaks, reforestation, carbon-binding, and timber production. Additionally, they sell "cap and trade" credits for carbon-neutralizing companies and contract 173 hectares with the Icelandic Forestry Association.
- **Sesseljuhus Environmental/Event Center**
  This is a popular venue for big-name concerts, creating revenue for Sólheimar. Like many other events that Sólheimar puts on, the public is willing to pay full price because they know that the money will go to a good cause.

  Sólheimar does have a highly regarded educational practice; they give talks at conferences and host tours of their facilities, both of which they make some revenue from.
- **Väla shop**
  Art, handmade wooden crafts, candles, value-added foods, etc. all generate revenue.
- **Græna Kannan Cafe**
  Sólheimar's lunches are very fresh, very local, and world-class. The baristas also know how to make world-class cappuccinos. I had one every day during my stay there.
- **Brekkukot Guesthouses**
  For rent on their website, guestrooms are affordable but are very profitable for Sólheimar.

Currently, Sólheimar is not a prosperous business venture per se, but it is contributing to the greater economy in more unassuming, sustaining ways. It also provides business services that society needs; there are extremely repetitive tasks that residents can (and like to) do for pharmaceutical companies that allow containers to be reused. This prevents excess waste in landfills, saves money, and creates jobs that are not easy for others to do. See Chapter 4.

***From the bylaws: Surplus income that may arise from the organization's activities goes to itself and shall be spent in accordance with its purpose and goals and the tasks that may fall under them according to this charter, incl. for projects organized by Sólheimar or the Endowment Fund Sólheima. Furthermore, the organization may receive other income or assets that may be at risk from individuals, associations or public bodies as a grant, gift, pledge, or inheritance. If there is a loss from the organization's activities, it must be paid from its funds or transferred to the following fiscal year.*

State social services also pay Sólheimar to employ people who are not otherwise employable. These people can be employed by Sólheimar, however, because they have learned how to subdivide complex jobs into basic components to create simple, repetitive tasks that the neurodivergent residents enjoy immensely.

At Sólheimar, a 30-year-old with autism can get a job—not only giving them pride and purpose but also providing enough money to pay for some of their own things like accommodations, snacks, hobbies, and amusement. For jobs to function in this community and feel rewarding and fulfilling to the neurodivergent folks, they almost always have to be broken down into their basic parts: I'll scrape the paint, you sand it, you prime it, and so on.

Support/Endowment Fund (Styrktarsjóður Sólheima)

The Support Fund of Sólheimar owns most of the buildings in Sólheimar. It collects rent from the residents and from the municipality for buildings used for servicing people with disabilities (workshops, the cantina, gym, etc.). Maintenance of buildings and all new buildings in Sólheimar are constructed by the Support Fund of Sólheimar.

Rent is paid by different means by each resident, such as disability income, work, or family. Teachers, social workers, and other professionals also have the option to live on-site. Professionals can live off-site but are encouraged to live at Sólheimar in order to be more deeply involved in the community (which almost all do).

The fund also includes:

- Social services for people with special needs
- Social housing operating cost

Loans from Government

- The support fund also holds all loans for the buildings and services the loans (some loans from the government have a special interest rate)

Partner Organizations

- The Lion's Club and the Blue Lagoon, for example, helped with the construction of supportive buildings

Donations and Gifts

- Donations and gifts go toward grants for practical projects and the purchase of tools or equipment in Sólheimar. They also provide staff and others with grants or loans for studies, as well as support for travel and leisure activities.

INTRODUCTION TO MANAGEMENT OF SÓLHEIMAR

Council of Representatives and Executive Board

Sólheimar is currently overseen by a 17-member representative council. Each year, they elect a five-member Executive Board (or "Commission"), on which each member serves a four-year term, with the opportunity to be re-elected. The Executive Board oversees major decisions and directions, and the Managing Director/CEO is in charge of day-to-day operations.[1]

Even with the considerable benefits that Sólheimar provides to the general population and to the Icelandic government, there are still lingering issues with local

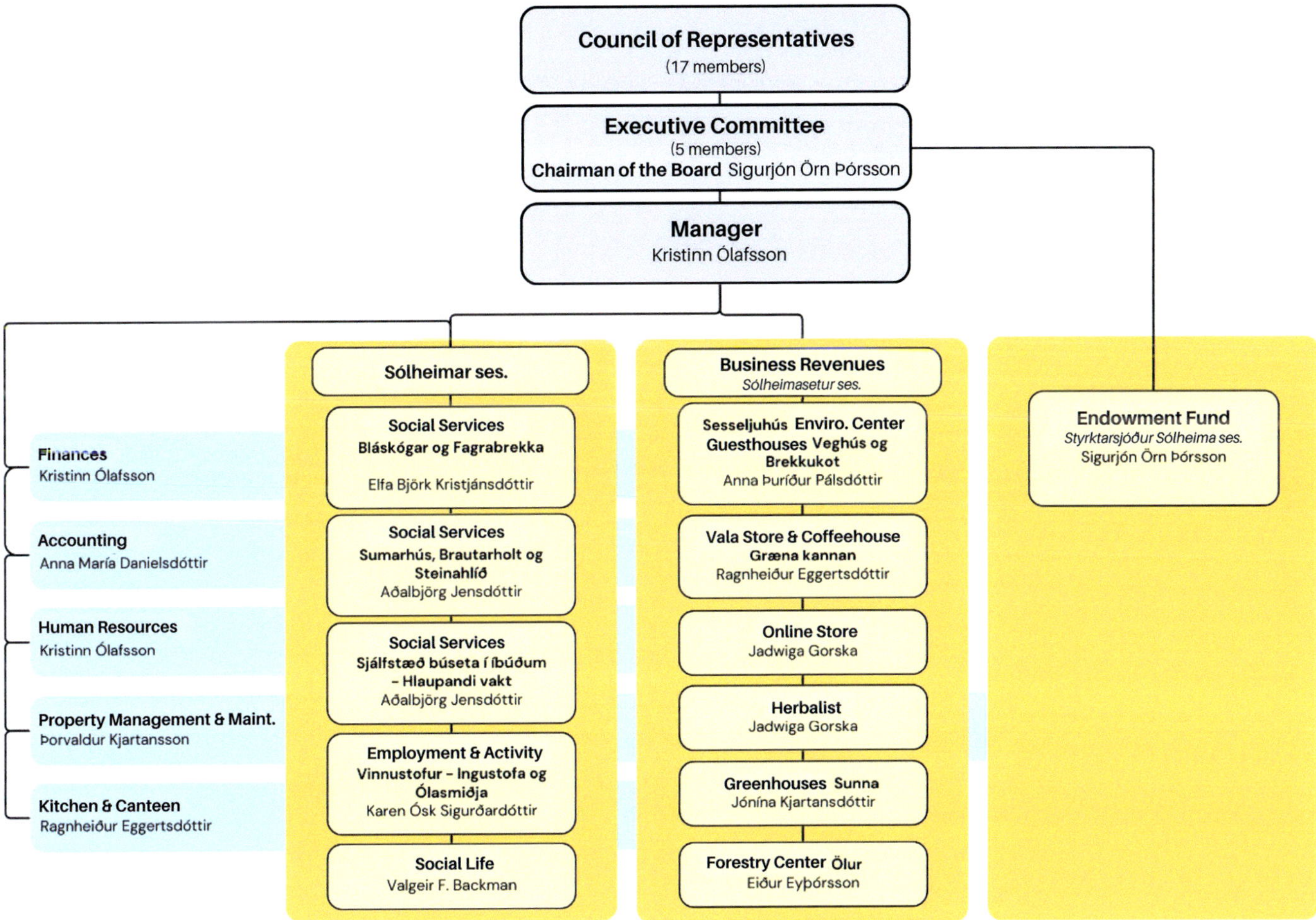

The Organization Chart of Sólheimar as of 2023.

municipalities. Sigurjón (Chairman of the Board) told us, "We are always overcoming obstacles. There are always some problems." They struggle each year to make financial ends meet and to keep their boat afloat. Luckily, the board of directors has considerable business expertise, and they also bring heart to the table.

Equitable, Inclusive, and Empowering Management Structures

Top-Down Management Creates Missed Opportunities

When I was visiting, I noticed that five dump trucks' worth of topsoil was being hauled off-site to make space for a concrete deck to be installed around the swimming pool. They were paying for the soil removal to be relocated off-site. I ran my hand through the black, humus-rich soil; I knew that this high-quality soil would be useful to the greenhouse crew, as they were in the process of purchasing some at a premium and were paying for the transportation of it to the site. The one thing that Iceland doesn't have is extra soil. I asked Piotr, the head manager of the greenhouse at the time if he had been asked

about this soil removal—a precious commodity on this island of lava. He said that he had not. He ran for his phone and called about it immediately, only to find out that it was too late.

I was curious about Piotr's work at Sólheimar running the 20+ greenhouses, so I inquired if he had ever been asked to join a management meeting by the senior managers or the Board of Directors. He said that he had not. When the folks on the ground are not included in management, important opportunities are missed, there is a huge loss of wisdom, and many good decisions are left on the table. True, cooperative ownership is lost.

Managing multi-facility operations is undeniably complex, but implementing a more horizontal management system can be immensely beneficial. This is currently a missed opportunity at Sólheimar. Management told me that in all the years of running the greenhouses, they have never "been in the black"—meaning it has never brought in more money than it spent. Although this is beginning to change, all the suggestions that the Greenhouse personnel and other workers could make to save money—such as transferring this expensive load of quality topsoil—are missed opportunities.

The board saw Sesselja operate with a top-down approach, and a system of more cooperative-based management style is yet to be fully adopted. They have several departments with many intelligent and dedicated employees; the entire operation would profit if all of their wisdom was valued and harnessed. There are consulting organizations that Sólheimar could hire to help them re-organize into a more cooperative, profitable establishment. At first, this outsourcing (consulting) may appear inefficient, but it has repeatedly proven to be a great way to achieve potential as an organization. Sometimes, you have to take one step back to take two steps forward; you have to build a cooperative organization in a deliberate fashion.

Fellowship facilitates management and encourages healthier self-management as well.

Many institutions operate with a top-down approach. This is to "protect the masses from themselves," so to speak. Employing experts to tackle complex challenges allows a less biased approach that comprehensively addresses the tasks at hand. It's an efficient strategy that can protect minority groups from being marginalized by overwhelming or oppressive majority voices. However, in the case of a small community like Sólheimar, a horizontal participatory system of governance or management would also be quite advantageous.

Participatory and Horizontal Management Structures

Participatory, horizontal management simply means that the leadership of an organization, community, or institution deliberately involves the members of that entity in its planning and operation. It is a system built on trust and mutual benefit, where avenues of communication are open and non-hierarchical. Research has shown that members involved in a participatory system have felt higher levels of autonomy, competency, and creativity in their work and consequently experience improved wellbeing and satisfaction.

There have been many interesting studies on participatory management within indigenous South American and African communities. When these communities adopt horizontal management approaches, problem-solving becomes significantly more efficient and gratifying. Oddly enough, another industry that is progressively implementing participatory systems is the small-scale fishing industry. Many countries are beginning to recognize that those on the boats can respond more efficiently and sustainably to the consistently changing demands of their trade than governmental regulatory bodies.

Non-Hierarchical Structure in Cohousing Communities (Co-Management)

I witness cohousing groups tap into the potential of participatory systems in monthly meetings. There is active, collective brainstorming and discussion that allows for problems to be solved by working toward a solution together. Cohousing math is 1+1=3. I have an idea, and you have an idea, but the idea we have together is the one that will allow us to reach our full potential. This non-hierarchical structure is a great management practice, as it allows for everyone to be included in the decision-making process. Not only do all the ideas get put on the table, but you learn how to pick the best one expeditiously. Most importantly, the emotional ownership in this system is concerned with accomplishing shared goals.

It would be great if a neurodiverse community could be managed like a neurotypical (if there is such a thing) cohousing community, but that is likely not possible. These communities probably need to practice a hybridized management approach where horizontal management is favored, but vertical tactics can be utilized when necessary. A pragmatic balance is likely needed to govern neurodiverse communities successfully.

Typical meeting in the common house of a cohousing community. See the short book Happily Ever Aftering in Cohousing for an in-depth description of the group process.

Co-creation makes a wonderful place; this new cohousing community is now built and functions very successfully. This is due to the fact that these 20 people each had a consequential say in its creation over the course of 12 full days of workshops to create design criteria and three months total of schematic design.

The same logic can be applied to a village community. Shared experiences, problems, and consented solutions offer an organic and efficient way of operating a village. Participation also saves time and money by avoiding redundancies, and it gives the residents a sense of ownership and autonomy. They become invested in the art of group problem-solving.

Some communities are already putting this inclusive, representative management structure into practice.

In the long run, however, communities like Sólheimar will likely always need to utilize a hybrid system where decisions are delegated to management, but people with boots on the ground are highly involved and influential in those decisions.

At some German neuro-inclusive communities, monthly meetings are held with all delegates from the various houses and workshops. This is a large co-management meeting for various communities around Germany.

Conclusion

The macroeconomics of places like Sólheimar provide a strong case for the benefits of community living with support systems in place. The calculations needed to prove that these communities would be economically beneficial are not currently performed in most cities, counties, states, or countries. The cost estimates and savings must be detailed and nuanced at the same time.

There are line items on both sides of the ledger (costs and revenue) that need to be recognized and deliberately calculated. South Korea's government performed an inspiring analysis by determining what BTS—a popular Korean boyband—added to their national GDP; they added about $4.9 billion, which amounted to 0.3% of the total GDP. Those are tricky and often unperformed economic calculations that consider hidden cost and revenue multipliers.

But, these analyses are achievable if we seek them out; there are many qualified economists capable of performing them. For Sólheimar, I would estimate the savings for governments and families of residents to be well over $30,000 per year per resident. It's not only about a singular, linear budget: "How do we get this place funded? Oh, it's too expensive." If you paint the bigger picture and consider the economic wellbeing of everyone—including the residents down the street, over the hilltop, and to the national borders beyond—economic feasibility becomes more attainable and attractive. Considerable administration costs become less burdensome when all the different means of income are considered: workshops; greenhouses; reforestation programs; housing allocations from the state; housing allocations from the facilities; housing income from the residents in conjunction with the resident jobs; education funding from the government; job training paid for by the state; care paid for by the government; income from selling products made on-site; income from the plays; etc. These economically beneficial components are also what make Sólheimar feel like an old-world village or even a modern-day village in Southern France; they make a difference, in many ways, to everyone.

In the end, investing in communities like this is more than worth it. When the governments, the local organizations, the board, the staff, and the local populations have values that align, solutions are inevitably found.

It's important to remember that Sólheimar was one person's dream over 90 years ago. All she had was her aspiration, her tenacity, a little money, and some help from her family. She put forward a plan: start with a site (her dad helped her negotiate a deal) and assemble volunteers to help determine physical access options for the remote site. She had to get approval to bring five orphans to come reside on-site with her (there were no buildings yet), garner volunteers to assemble tents to live in for the summer, and volunteers to construct a building for the winter. She had to find people to help her apply for grants from private donors, governments, private corporations, and churches. But she did it all. All of this should not be intimidating; the first step is simply to get started as Sesselja did, and the rest will fall into place. You must begin with an overarching goal and a simple plan. The complexity will grow as your capacity to manage complexity increases. Becoming an activist and an organizer will allow you to overcome economic barriers successfully.

Perhaps the macroeconomics question is, "What happens to an economy when ten to 15% of the population who have not been working start to work—and love it?" There is no doubt that a more hybrid, individualized system can generate the energy to make a project efficient. Sure, Sólheimar could be more efficient; the inefficiencies are not intentional. Everybody wants to conserve and think through the details, but everybody also deserves to be heard. The system needs to be more participatory in every aspect, from saving money to saving the planet and everything in between.

This chapter about money and management is probably the least translatable to other programs. This proforma (revenue in and revenue out) and management will be different for every project.

Note

[1] *A little history: "After Sesselja's death, the National Church's Children's Home Committee appointed representatives to a five-member board. In 1987, an amendment was made to Sólheima's charter and a representative council was established with 21 representatives. Sólheima's charter was changed in 2004 and the number of representatives was reduced from 21 to 17. The council elects a five-member executive committee from among the representative councilors at the general meeting."*

CHAPTER 9

Honoring everyone, every sound, is the beginning and the end of a healthy social life. Where there is disrespect, there is lingering sorry.

Other Neuro-Inclusive Communities

There are many other programs around the world dedicated to assisting the neurodivergent population in achieving more fulfilling and fruitful lives. Many of the insights offered in this book specifically describe how cohousing and community are both feasible and therapeutic for this population. This book focuses on Sólheimar because their 94-year evolution serving people with autism and Down syndrome has taught us many valuable lessons. We cannot speak to the specific diagnoses served in other communities, but many of the same concepts have the potential to apply successfully. Since Sólheimar's inception, they have evolved into an ecovillage: a self-sufficient place where everyone lives, works, and shops. It, therefore, operates more like a village than an institution or a housing establishment designed exclusively for the caretaking of these populations, where there are "employees" and "patients."

DOI: 10.4324/9781003642336-10

There are numerous other communities forming, and different models and solutions are percolating in the U.S. Many developments are underway, and new organizations are starting to form. We can't mention all of the archetypes in this book, but we will mention a few so that you can be inspired by the current momentum. A great resource is the Autism Housing Network; through this network, you can find a country-wide Housing Directory. They also recently published a very useful report called "A Place in the World: Fueling Housing and Community Options for Adults with Autism and Other Neurodiversities." What we do know is that there are millions of people with autism and Down syndrome who are isolated—and we aspire to change this.

Though Sólheimar may be one of the oldest, many other neuro-inclusive communities around the world have been established in recent decades. They have embraced true community as a means of setting neurodivergent people up for success. They offer a place where acquaintances can become best friends, a place where relationships turn into kinships, and a place where purpose is a key objective. They offer a place where residents can have 25–35 hours of meaningful peer interaction per week. They offer a place where romance has the opportunity to flourish, which can play a role in achieving a full life. They provide a place where every individual who wants purpose has purpose; where they can make things and break things; where people can express themselves fully. The rest of the world considers failure to be an integral part of success, essential to growth, learning, and self-improvement. Many of the residents at Sólheimar have become true artisans and have gained immense pride from that—resulting in full, rewarding, and satisfying lives. The community of Sólheimar indeed exemplifies a successful neuro-inclusive cohousing community. And we know that creating a solution is possible in every town and region across the world.

Essence of Community

Community is an integral, integrated set of relationships that is the currency of consequence when it comes to a rich life.

Community is where people know each other and care about each other. Community is where people support each other.

How Do They Know Each Other?

They work together, they cook together, and they gather for meals. They take swimming lessons together, they go for hikes together, they clear brush together, they are in the play, dances, and choir together, they have leisure time together, and they perpetually communicate together.

How Do They Care About Each Other?

They ask how one another is doing, they listen to each other's woes, and they learn about each other's pasts. Proximity necessitates care. I personally live in a 34-unit cohousing community; every adult in the community is required to cook dinner once a month. Two residents team up and cook together, and it is typical for your co-chef to be different each time. Once, I made dinner with Sim; we cooked a complicated Indian meal together for the entire community. Neither of us had made that type of meal before. Prior to cooking together, my ideas about Sim stemmed from his consistently puzzling and enigmatic comments in the community meetings. But I came to find that he was thoughtful, thorough, and patient, and dinner was a huge success. I got to know Sim more intimately that night and learned what a great person he really is. We did something of consequence together; I have given him the benefit of the doubt ever since that evening. These consequential acts create bonding opportunities; they bring people in a village together.

How Do They Support Each Other?

They make sure to bring each other chicken soup when one of them has a cold. They prepare breakfast and coffee for each other; they help get each other going in the morning. They support each other like new-found family, like new-found friends. They help each other like only a non-paid caregiver could. This is not an obligation—they don't do it because they must but because they want to. They know that it will all come back to them someday when they need it.

Identity

Community is a proud sense of identity: "I live in *that* community." Community is a warm sense of belonging:

> *I belong here, I want to be here, I love it here, I'm proud of this place, and I'm proud of myself and/or my family for helping me figure out that I would be better off here than elsewhere. I'm proud of my community because they helped me figure out who I am in this place; they helped me figure out how to live here happily.*

Purpose and Mutual Management

Community aids and increases production, improving skills through mentorship and co-creation to help each other become skilled craftsmen and artisans. Community optimizes self-management (of my own affairs) and mutual management (of *our* affairs), proving that mutual management is a stronger and smarter tactic because you have the brains of others contributing—and those perspectives percolate into the care we give to ourselves individually. In Community, 1+1 = 3. I have an idea, you have an idea, and together, we not only come up with the best third idea, but we are also more likely to get it done and actualize a plan.

We are driven by bias and self-doubt when thinking and brainstorming in isolation. Combine those mental blocks with a little inertia and we often become stuck and are unlikely to actualize a thoughtful plan at all. We are stronger together, in a community.

Case Studies of Other Neuro-Inclusive Communities

Anthroposophical Inspired Communities in Europe

Hertha Levefællesskab

Examples of Neuro-Inclusive Communities in the U.S.

WeBUILT (We Build Unique Independent Lives Together)

Creative Living Community of CT

International Foundations Dedicated to the Founding of Neuro-Inclusive Communities

L'Arche Communities

A Note on Anthroposophy

Anthroposophy, as it is recognized today, is a holistic philosophy rooted in human development that emphasizes our independence from the pressures and standards society places on us. Fundamentally, it's a spiritual movement guided by the teachings of the 19th-century German philosopher and architect Rudolf Steiner. Today, it guides the humanity-centered approach to insight in self-expression through deep awareness. It helps us study human nature and development. Anthroposophy's etymology comes from the Greek words for human (Anthropos) and wisdom (Sophia). It concludes that there is an inherent wisdom within us that, once cultivated, can help us navigate the complexities of life.

This is very important in the context of many preexisting neuro-inclusive communities. If there is an inherent, spiritual foundation that connects and equalizes all of us universally, then what is classified as "developmentally disabled" or "neurodivergent" is only a condition of the body and says nothing about the value of the individual. Therefore, neuro-inclusive communities embrace the inherent equal value in all individuals and allow for growth and development in the presence of one another. This development is enabled through our relationships, creativity, and connection with surrounding environments and ecologies. These communities broadly follow anthroposophical principles, though each is unique in character and operation. Such is the case with Sólheimar. We expound upon the discipline of anthroposophy because so many diverse communities rely on it to bring out their best intentions. It guides them to value the equality and wholeness of all people; it encourages them to elevate the uniqueness of individuals and the realization of their potential.

Hertha Levefællesskab ("Living Community")

Community Near Aarhus, Denmark

Location: Denmark

Organization: Single Village with 18 homes, 10 condominiums, 25 rental units

Population: 150 total residents, 27 with disabilities, 40 staff

Operating Philosophy
Hertha originated as a foundation with a focus on collectivism, biodynamic agriculture, ecological activism, cultural transformation through youth involvement, and assisting people with learning disabilities. Here, the ingredients for a quality life are universal, whether you have a developmental disability or not. Guided by the anthroposophical philosophies of Rudolf Steiner, the cooperation of disabled and non-disabled people (they call it "reverse integration") in this small village improves the quality of *all* lives. At Hertha, they adhere to the following principles for a healthy, reciprocal community:

1. A safe, casual, routine environment.
2. Meaningful work and good nutrition.
3. A diverse social life with opportunities for creative expression.
4. An individual-focused learning atmosphere that promotes freedom and independence.

If these can be balanced by the individual and by the community, then the "whole person" can be developed and can master everyday life.

Village Characteristics

Hertha operates on 50 acres (20 hectares) of land, combining life and work through opportunities to participate in around 35 workshops in the community. Everyone can find something that meets their needs in a holistic manner, whether it's labor-driven, creativity-driven, therapeutic, or fulfilling in another way. Aside from work, the community gathers for routine social and cultural events. The village dinner is held every other week; the sale of handmade goods happens at seasonal markets; relaxing after a day's work at the common house is a daily occurrence—there's always an opportunity to connect with each other. Building confidence and developing the skills necessary to work with others is important here, so every Wednesday, the village gathers to rehearse and eventually perform a play. So far, they have produced over 120 live performances. Theatre provides the environment to challenge yourself through engagement and creativity. Everyone feels accomplished after the final show.

Food Production at Hertha Levefællesskab

60-acre (25-hectare) Hertha Farm:

- ½ dedicated to grazing
- ½ dedicated to rye, oats, and wheat
- 9 dairy cows
- 3 beehives

Dairy:

- 600 liters of milk produced per week, sold in Aarhus

3-acre (1¼-hectare) Garden and Greenhouse:

- Lettuce, carrots, potatoes, tomatoes, vegetables, and herbs

Farming together.

At the bakery, they make all kinds of breads, cakes, buns, gluten-free options, and muesli—much of which they sell.

Paintings are displayed at local cafes and as backdrops for theatre performances.

Theatre is integral.

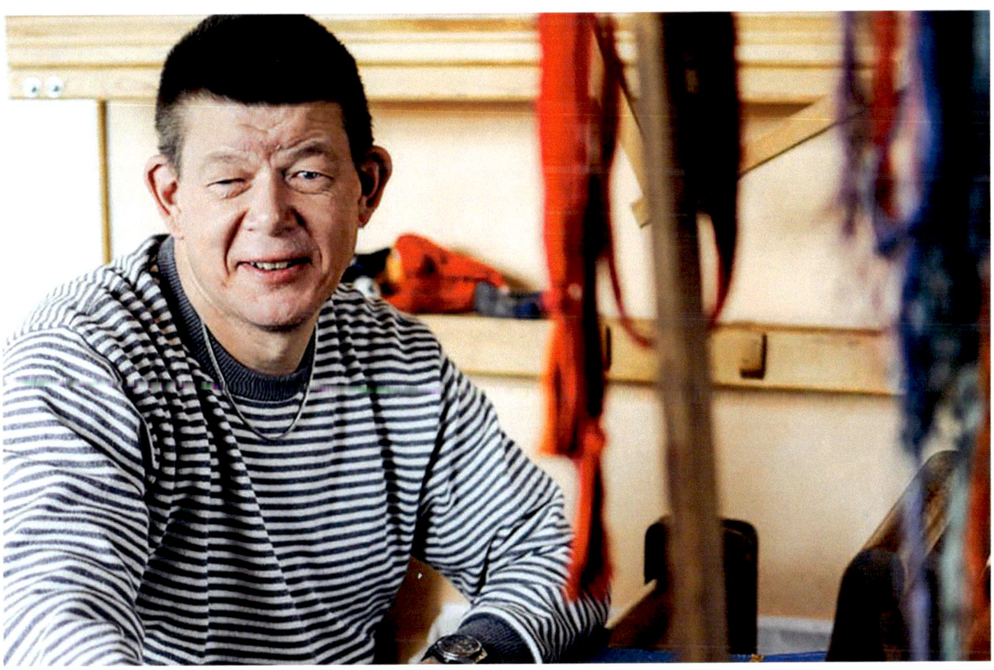

Handicrafts include blankets, cushions, fine bags, towels, and scarves.

Examples of Neuro-Inclusive Communities in the U.S.

WeBUILT (We Build Unique Independent Lives Together)

Location: First community built in Clackamas, OR

Phase: Additional communities in development

Community: 35 individual homes, one common house

Non-Profit Organization: Next Step Strategies, Inc.

Axon rendering by Communitecture.

WeBUILT is a privately owned cohousing-inspired community with 35 individual homes and a large community space called the Party Barn (aka Common House). Their goal is to provide healthy living with opportunities for leisure, recreation, and volunteer activities while promoting and advocating for choice and independence. The first example community was built in Clackamas, Oregon. Additional communities are being developed in Missouri, Texas, California, and North Carolina.

Creative Living Community of CT

Location: Manchester, Connecticut

Phase: In development

Community: 50 residents, 1-, 2-, 3-, and 4-bedroom homes

Non-Profit Organization: Creative Living Community of CT, Inc.

This farm community, intended for about 50 adults, both with and without developmental disabilities, is currently in development. The idea is that by living, working, and socializing together, individuals will discover a sense of belonging and purpose in life. Plans for the community include private, market-rate homes on ten acres of land.

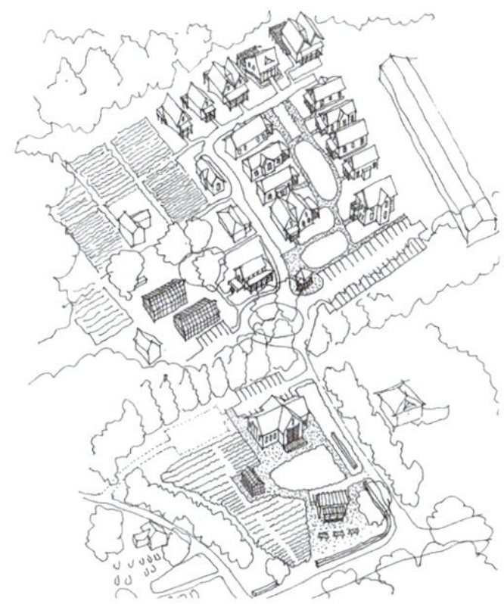

Aerial sketch by Union Studio.

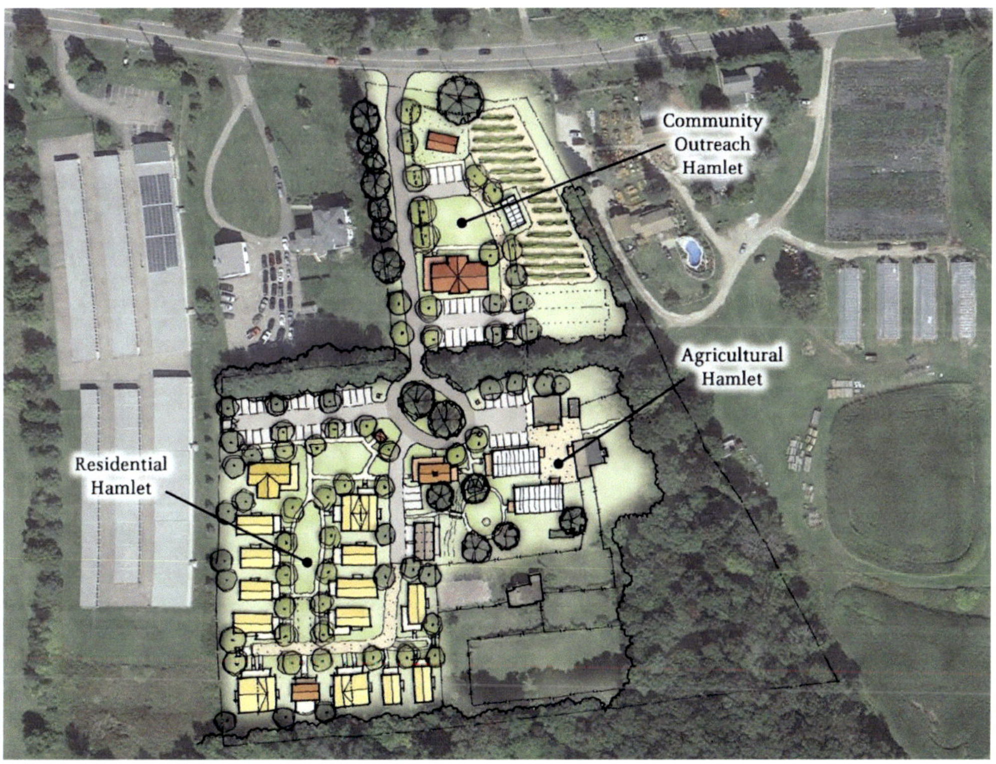

Village Site Plan.

International Movements Dedicated to Establishing Neuro-Inclusive Communities

L'Arche is an international movement dedicated to creating inclusive communities for people with and without disabilities to live integrated lives. Their individual sub-communities vary greatly in form.

L'Arche International

L'Arche is an international federation of non-profit organizations specializing in the creation of communities that accommodate and integrate people with and without intellectual disabilities. They originated in France over 50 years ago in response to institutions and the inhumane conditions that people with disabilities endured. L'Arche has created over 150 communities in over 38 countries around the world.

L'Arche operates under the philosophy of "with," not "for," emphasizing that individuals with and without disabilities should have equal opportunities to contribute to society. L'Arche communities are guided by the principles of Christianity, yet they are continually influenced and enriched by diverse faiths, beliefs, and spiritual practices. Making connections through shared goals and spirituality, residents integrate, creating friendships through the common ideals they share within the community.

Take Inspiration and Learn from Existing Programs

We don't recommend that any new program attempts to copy an existing one. You could travel the world, spend countless dollars and years doing so, and still be unable to design a successful project. Studying precedents in this way is interesting and entertaining, but it's not particularly useful. You'd have to understand the very specific issues of each program—the Icelandic culture, the improvised Mexican economy, or other distinct characteristics and limitations—to know what's appropriate in each case. Sólheimar is a great start as a model because they have succeeded at creating an inclusive community that exemplifies healthy interpersonal relationships while concurrently valuing individual sense of purpose. They have stood the test of time, and they weren't copying anyone. They dug deep to figure out who they are, who they aspire to be, and exactly what the process is to get there.

What Sólheimar grew quite organically over 94 years—based on their unique identity and goals—was done so with consistent intentionality and introspection, and they made mistakes along the way (see the next chapter on how to set yourself up for success). It is critical to ask yourself, "Who are we? And who exactly do we want to become?" There are methodologies that get the work done much faster, more economically, and create a more integrated environment than Sólheimar. It wasn't until 1974 that Sesselja figured out and implemented better housing arrangements for many of the residents. New housing was built as small, shared row homes designed specifically to house four residents and one social worker in each. This finally turned out to be the right answer for Sólheimar. That has worked fantastically (see Chapter 3)—but it took them 44 years to figure it out. Successful design can be implemented from the beginning if specific goals are defined, composition is carefully calculated, and the process is intentional and participatory. We have a poster in our office that says, "If it doesn't work socially, why bother?" The worst cohousing projects are those that mimic the best ones; different places, different people, different towns, and different subcultures each require specific, deliberate, thoughtful, and unique design processes. Taking "shortcuts"—imitating other projects—can result in ineffective solutions for the urgent, critical problem of serving an immense suffering population with neurodiversity.

CHAPTER 10

The good that we secure for ourselves is as much the life between the buildings as much as it is the life within the buildings and the common life we build together.

Next Steps: How to Get a Neuro-Inclusive Cohousing Started in Your Town

Despite how inspiring the story of Sesselja is—and how she brought her concept of Sólheimar to life—this book does not advocate following her footsteps. Rather, we should learn from her lessons, use Sólheimar as a point of departure, and launch from where she landed. Sesselja didn't take no for an answer when she was denied by the bureaucrats, and neither should you. Let her vision and passion inspire you and your colleagues; conceive your own dream village through a tested, deliberate process. This chapter could be interpreted as somewhat of a formula—a formula with Sesselja's imprint and the imprint of many others. Although the growth of a project should be somewhat organic, as Sesselja's was, it needs to be more calculated and meticulous to be truly successful. And the success of these projects is crucially—and urgently—depended upon by those in need.

DOI: 10.4324/9781003642336-11

There really is no singular "formula," per se—other than tenacity and grass roots organizing—but there are very specific processes to get projects on this scale built. It's not just about paid consultant work. The big WHY that drove me to write this book is because I want to see a few families in need get together and create a local solution for their kids using a smart, deliberate, participatory, and responsive process. It's not about a "formula" as much as it's about the motivation and the collaboration required to do it properly and efficiently.

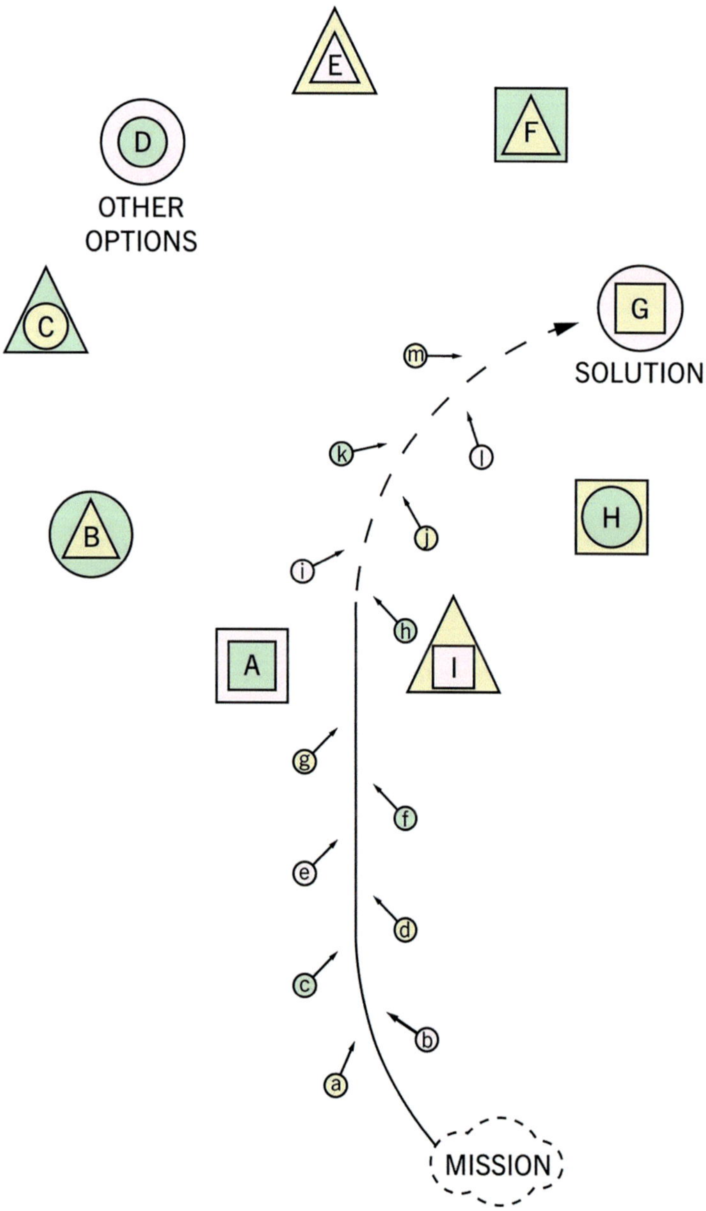

This is not about reinventing the wheel—it is very much about *understanding* your wheel. This book is meant to empower you to have the confidence to simply begin your process: to start with understanding who you are and exactly where it is that you want to go. The process need not start from "scratch"; in a proper process, you start with a blank sheet of paper and—with guidance—can devise a cohesive plan in a matter of days. At The Cohousing Company, we have programmed 55 cohousing communities in days, large schools in days—even a small clinic (for Patch Adams) in days—because we knew every question that needed to be asked, from small to large.

Goals: to have everyone belong, etc. (x50)

Activities: to play, etc. (x150)

Places: seating for ten, comfortability, material, etc. (x1000)

Programming is complicated; it is necessarily the basis of design, and it understands the intent of the client(s) and the behaviors they would like to see. The architect must come back and say, "This covers the intent," or, "This does not fit."

Why it doesn't work to copy other programs:

1. People don't want to discuss their mistakes, and they especially don't want to talk about missed considerations in their design processes. I don't even recommend reviewing other projects' program documents; too much time can be spent investigating and evaluating. Why did they do this? Why not that? If anything,

look at their program (design criteria) once you have made progress on yours to imagine what you might be leaving out—usually, this does not lead to new insights—because you've already learned how to complete your own criteria—but it can occasionally be helpful.

2. Too much time is spent on evaluating other designs, and past mistakes rarely provide coherent criteria.
3. The program diagram on the previous page shows that if you put all of your criteria (a, b, c, d) together from all of the stakeholders, consultants, etc., in a deliberate fashion, it will successfully lead to your solution (in this case G). No one else has done your G before. Evaluating another project's A, B, C, D, E, F, etc., to see what they got wrong or right can be ceaseless, and it doesn't produce the project that *you* need. The most famous instance of this happened in a cohousing project in Denmark that copied a very high-functioning cohousing (also in Denmark). The imitation project turned out to be a very low-functioning community.

The development process of every cohousing will be somewhat unique. In some cases, the core group establishes its goals and priorities before identifying a site, but we recommend specifying a specific site together first, if possible. It's best to work with a professional who has navigated this type of project before, can help put a team together, and can provide clear criteria. During the development process, the following steps laid out in this chapter should take place (although the timing and sequence will vary).

But before we start, I want to point out that a fundamental building block of an ecovillage is a cohousing community. Cohousing forces a group to become very deliberate in their decision-making process. Goals for the cohousing process are well-defined and easy to implement, as they are thorough, fair, and thoughtful—they are not random. Furthermore, by creating a cohousing community first, you establish the foundational sense of village through proximity and connections. This allows the other supportive components of an ecovillage—such as farms, gardens, and cafes—to follow, even if they were the impetus for the project at the onset. Creating the cohousing community first breaks the project into manageable phases.

This chapter very much intends to provide the necessary steps to create *your* best place that will provide your community with what they need to go forward and develop their best selves. To figure out exactly what behaviors and environment you want, envision a world that facilitates those goals.

This chapter delineates the key steps. From my experience of creating and co-creating 55 cohousing communities and hundreds of other living arrangements, I have learned that one must determine how to get exactly where one wants to go through a very intentional process.

Please keep in mind that every project is unique, and nuances abound; the following sections of this chapter are not necessarily sequential, but it is nonetheless recommended that these steps be taken deliberately.

Alternate Approach

- Find a site
- Make an offer
- Have a public presentation

Keep in mind that every project can start with just one motivated person who dreams of living in a high-functioning and supportive community. From there, they can build momentum and recruit like-minded individuals through public presentations or the GIB Workshop, and eventually bring their shared vision to life through the design workshops.

PRELIMINARY DEVELOPMENT PHASE

1. Develop an Umbrella Organizing Group through the *Getting-it-Built* workshop (The Cohousing Company) and/or through friends, acquaintances, and collaborators. This group will assist with understanding local interests and contexts and help you to get to know other people who share your goals and priorities. At this early stage, it is advantageous to function as an "umbrella" group that accommodates people with varied interests rather than dispersing the group energy into specific core groups. This organizing group can:

- Generate local interest in the concept
- Educate the public and local officials
- Get books like this one broadly distributed
- Build community support
- Gather information about markets and local opportunities
- Hold consistent meetings to keep the project progressing

Developing an effective working structure is the Umbrella Organizing Group's first order of business. This includes:

- A clearly defined Statement of Purpose, i.e., "Build a community for the neurodiverse population" (I would start with folks with mid-range autism, Down syndrome, or a specific I/DD subgroup)
- An organizational structure: committees and coordination
- A meeting structure: facilitation, agendas, minutes, etc.
- Defined purpose of different meeting types: general meetings, committee meetings, social functions, business meetings, discussions
- An internal communication network: a whole group listserv, committee listservs, etc.
- External communication network: newsletters and a database of contacts. Speaking at churches, neurodiverse conferences, etc.
- Decision-making procedures

It is important, however, not to put an organization together just for

An early public presentation with everyone invited: politicians, parents, developers, neighbors, supporters, and other parties. Thursday nights are a good time to schedule presentations; plan on 100–200 attendees. Invite them to a Saturday morning meeting at the library for a follow-up discussion. Thirty to 40 will predictably come to that.

A Saturday morning follow-up meeting at the library. If you don't have a site, get organized to find one. Explain what the getting-it-built workshop is and let other participants know that many cohousing projects have been initiated through this workshop. It only takes two things to make a community: a vision and a clear set of steps.

the sake of having one. The main objective is to get traction and make progress in a deliberate fashion. Since we started this book, I have more or less begun every day with the awareness that there are people with disabilities waiting to move into a supportive environment in their town. We highly recommend that the group hires a professional like The Cohousing Company to facilitate a *Getting-It-Built (GIB)* workshop, which outlines:

The Development Process

- An overview of the development process: from initial meetings to move-in
- Development scenarios and party roles: the group's roles, consultant's roles, and options for finding and working with a developer

The Technical Issues

- Money: getting your money in and getting your money out
- Financing options: ownership structures and financial realities (what will it cost?)
- How to stay on budget
- Relationships to governmental bodies: support from public health and social service.

Working Together

- How does the group organize to make decisions effectively?
- Getting along: the dynamics of group interaction, how to reach your potential

What's Next?

- Am I ready? What do we do now? Next steps: establish clear roles
- Your role; the group's role; the role of professionals moving forward

Begin Process

- How the group reaches its potential to establish a great community
- What does the efficient, quality, and cost-conscious design process look like overall?

Don't assume that because there is no "for sale" sign at the site that it's not for sale. These are often the best sites because the landowner will usually be more flexible with terms.

2. Site Criteria, Evaluation, and Acquisition

Identify Site Criteria, *specifically:*

- Geographic preferences
- Individual financial capabilities and target price range for dwellings
- Desired amenities of the surrounding area (i.e., schools, public transportation, neighborhood shopping, parks, and recreation areas)
- Preferred zoning densities
- Acceptable neighborhood character

Don't assume that because there are buildings on the site, it is not available. Its highest and best use very well might be new community/cohousing buildings and/or repurposed structures and infill that could form an ecovillage.

In addition to utilizing questionnaires and hosting group discussions, it is often useful to take field trips to see sample sites and existing cohousing. The group will learn a great deal about their own preferences on field trips, but only when they have already established their own specific criteria. It is helpful to learn more about what is realistic and to understand that trade-offs may be required in order to achieve your goals. You may find that there are competing criteria among the Umbrella Organizing Group's members; it is therefore helpful to keep a database of site criteria and priorities.

Select a Site

Once a potential site is identified, the group (often acting through an agent) will negotiate a purchase option that allows time to research the site thoroughly. Zoning; master plans for the area; the possibility and process of increasing the density; soil (potential for toxic wastes); structural integrity of existing buildings; financial feasibility; neighborhood concerns; and the owner's objectives all need to be thoroughly investigated. This information will be used to negotiate the price and terms of purchase with the owner of the site. The purchase option "ties up" the site for a few months so that no one else can buy it while the group researches its feasibility for the proposed project and seeks planning approvals. In some cases, the site is purchased only after the planning approvals are granted.

DESIGN PROCESS FOR A NEW ECOVILLAGE

1. Getting-It-Built Workshop/ Feasibility Study

The first step is to examine the aspects that determine the project's feasibility and establish the best strategy for moving forward. This is assisted by tools such as the working feasibility site plan. The following should be explored in the ongoing feasibility study:

- What is the best strategy for developing the project on this site?
- What are the optimal sizes and building types? Will specific design possibilities work?
- Budget and scope of the project: is the proposed project financially viable?
- Site analysis: zoning, utilities, drainage, etc.
- Is the site structurally sound? What is the soil capacity? What will be required regarding soil testing, seismic upgrades, etc.?
- How will other site considerations—such as sound levels, traffic, trees, grade, etc.—affect the project?
- Are there any toxins or hazardous materials to be dealt with?
- What are the preliminary civil engineering questions (paving, grading, drainage, etc.) and structural engineering questions (structural system, soils, etc.)?
- Are there any environmental concerns? Wetlands? Delicate ecosystems?
- Can staff reach the property, or will they have difficulty getting to work? Will staff housing be provided?
- Is there at least one service provider in the area that shares your values and can offer long-term support services to residents?
- What other costs, planning, and design constraints might the project encounter?

By addressing these questions up front, you can avoid costly and frustrating surprises down the road.

The *GIB* workshop will outline a legal process (starting with an LLC) and a financial process (from funding to allocation), establish a site, and lastly, facilitate a design process.

Buying a site is rarely done by consensus; usually, it comes down to who's ready to negotiate a mutually beneficial agreement.

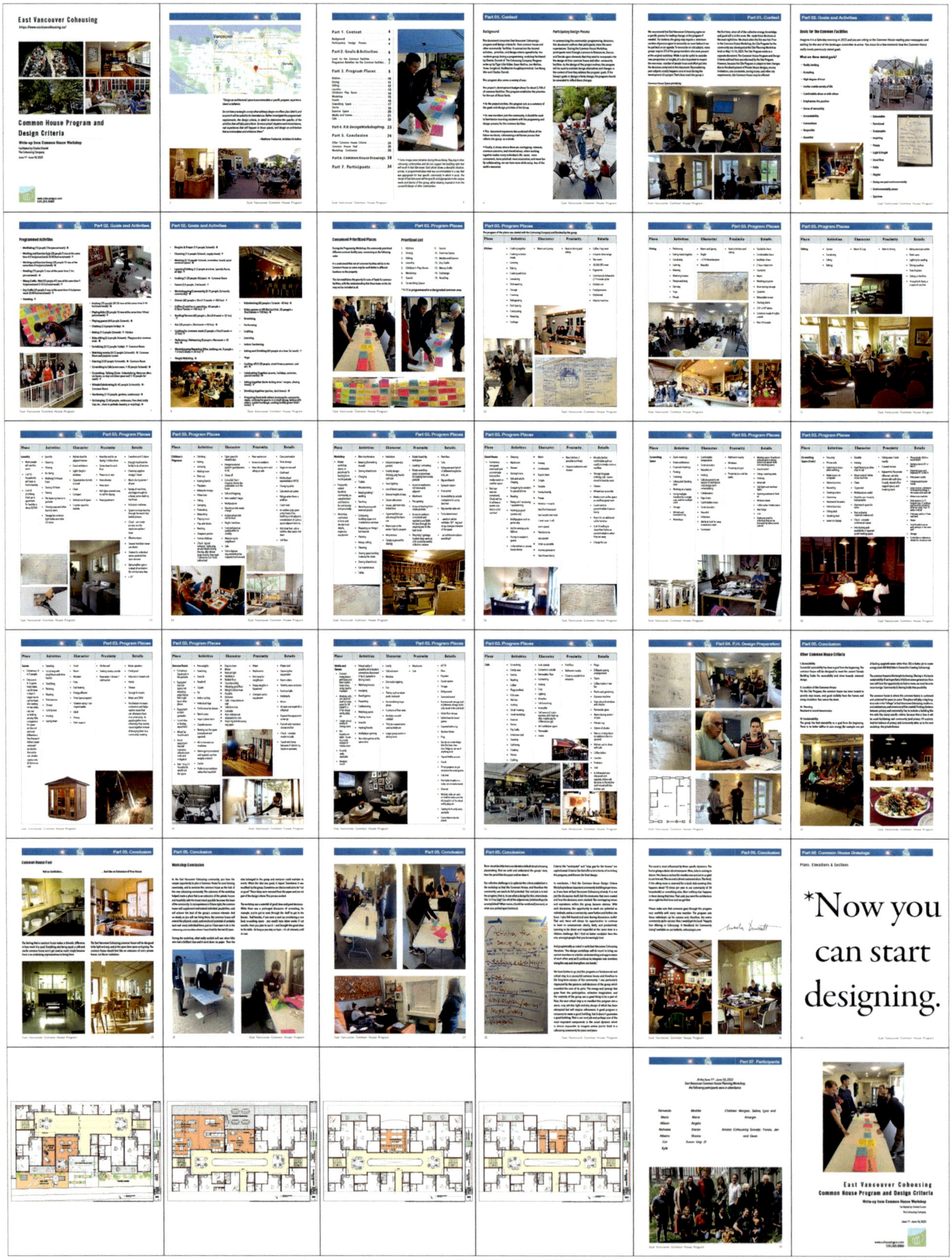

A sample program write-up for the commons of a cohousing community in East Vancouver, BC. From goals to activities and spaces, this document embodies the vision and spirit of the community, as well as the specific design criteria that the future residents co-created during the participatory design workshop. See the book Cohousing Communities for six sample programs. However, I want to again emphasize the importance of establishing your own criteria, independent from other projects.

2. Site Programming (Establishing Criteria for Site Design)

As mentioned in Chapter 3: The Architecture of Sólheimar, programming is the process used to arrive at the set of criteria on which the design will be based and evaluated. The programming phase is where the project is built—not *brick by brick*, but *decision by decision*. This is the time when a common vocabulary for the project is created and when preferences and requirements are determined and incorporated into the overall picture—before time is invested in design. It is when you, the future inhabitants, truly understand *who you are, who you aspire to be, and how your future neighborhood can support your ultimate goal and vision*.

What will the site plan look like? A village? One building? What will the various common facilities look like? Dining, support services, counseling offices, etc.? What will the housing arrangement be?

One of the most important purposes of the program is to reduce the need for later backtracking, redesign, and added costs. Another important function of programming is to begin the process of building a tight-knit community. It *must* involve future residents; their participation crucially contributes to getting the criteria correct.

During the programming process, we go through a detailed list of criteria, looking for program needs that translate into size, location, and other design requirements and qualities. This is particularly important when you are designing a community for a neurodiverse population, as these spatial qualities need to accommodate the sensory sensitivities that people with cognitive differences experience on a daily basis.

Goals, Activities, and Places: all created by the future residents for their future community. These decisions build the physical community. The relationships formed in the workshops—along with the appropriate contextual environmental design—are the foundations of a high-functioning community.

Moving blocks around in these workshops create relationships that are reinforced by the physical design for many years to come.

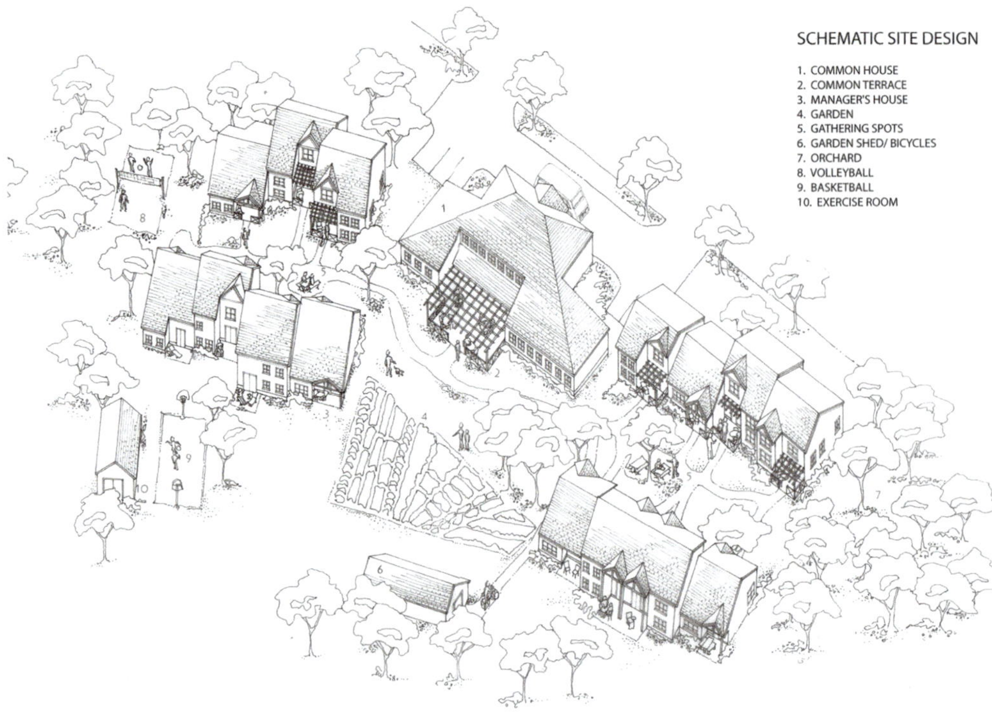

Homestead Friends Foundation Cohousing: *17-unit cohousing designed for people with a variety of diagnoses, from Williams syndrome to Down syndrome. The goal was to create an environment where the adult children could be coached to achieve independence in a supportive community. It was also designed to have no paid staff on site. This community was designed for residents of 70–90 IQ and was created next to another collaborative effort for residents of 50–70 IQ. Neither community was funded by the state of California at the time; I believe that they were not funded because they were considered "overreaching" for their time. The pedagogy is shifting, and neurodiverse communities are becoming more accepted now. This project was planned exclusively with the parents of the residents and the Cohousing Company.*

To create thorough site design criteria for neurodiverse communities, some questions that architects ask future residents can include but are not limited to:

- How are gathering nodes regularly dispersed on the site? What specific spatial qualities should they have to convey a sense of welcoming and belonging?
- Will there be places along the site that act as escape spaces for when one feels overstimulated? What specific spatial qualities should they have to convey a sense of protection and calm?
- Where should the common house be located? Does it provide close proximity and sight visibility to each of the private houses?
- Where will the workshop(s) be located? How are they grouped or clustered together? Do their locations provide enough sensory separation from the residents' private spaces?
- Will the site have a designated open space? How big does it need to be?

Nevada City Cohousing: *The site layout is designed so that spontaneous interactions between neighbors are not only possible but also feel natural and welcomed.*

During the process, the architect of the project will make recommendations based on their experience and professional knowledge. All the requirements of the project are then articulated and organized clearly in a written program, which will be a key reference throughout the design process.

The site programming finalizes the residents' goals and criteria for the physical layout of their community. The result is a preliminary site plan that documents the location of buildings, parking, gardens, play areas, gathering areas, and an architectural "program" that demonstrates the group's goals and criteria for the project.

3. Common Facility Programming and Schematic Design Workshop
The Common House Programming Workshop establishes the goals and priorities for the common house, where most of the common facilities and amenities—including a common kitchen and common dining room—are located. The architect should work closely with the group to define the goals of the common house and the specific activities taking place there and subsequently define the design criteria for each space individually. The purpose of this programming is not to "design" the common house but rather to establish specific agreed-upon guidelines as the basis for the design that will be drawn up later.

To create thorough common space design criteria for neurodiverse communities, some questions that architects ask future residents can include but are not limited to:

- How many people do we expect to show up at one common dinner? How often do common meals happen? There are no "ideal" numbers.
- What activities do we expect to do before and after the meal? Do these activities need their own specific spaces, and can they be located near the common dining space? Will there be any sensory transitions between them?
- How many guest rooms are we proposing? Will any of the rooms be reserved for specific caretakers?
- Will there be any offices in the common house for social workers?

It requires very deliberate prioritization to get the necessary facilities built and not to overspend. Our favorite scenario is when these workshops include parents, funders, and even future residents.

Once the workshop is complete, the architect should produce complete documentation of all decisions that the group has reached a consensus on (typically around 400 decisions). The architect will then develop the schematic floor plans and elevations based on the program, submit them to the group, and amend them as directed—creating plans that accurately reflect the group's decisions.

(Top Left) ***Nevada City Cohousing*** *Common House*

(Right) ***La Querencia Cohousing*** *Common House Plan*

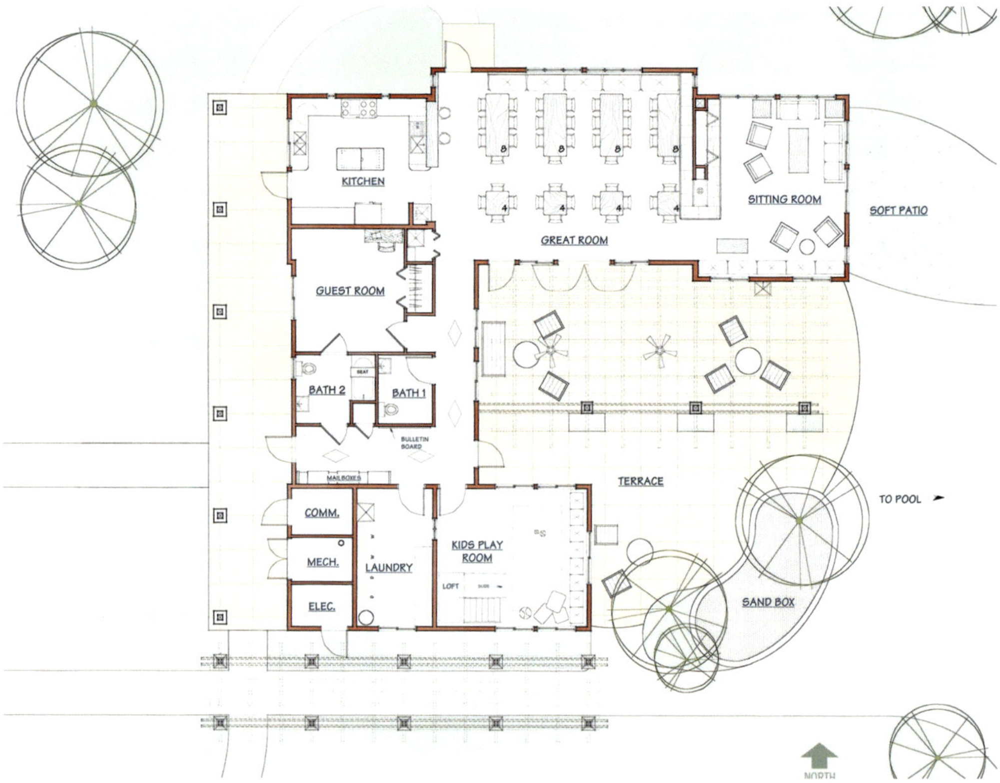

Quimper Village Cohousing *Common House Plan*

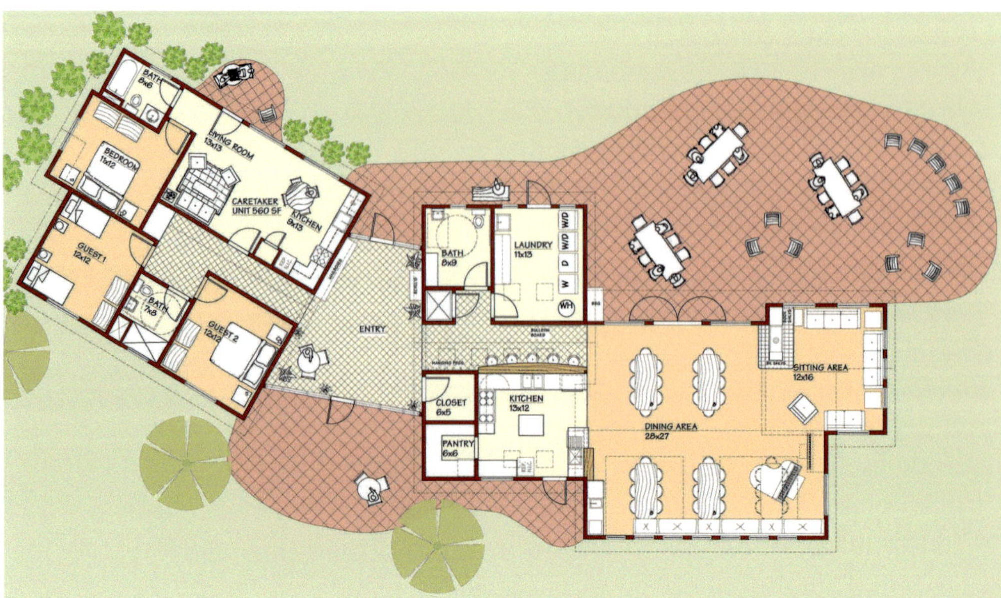

4. Private House Programming and Schematic Design Workshop

In the Private House Programming Workshop, the architect meets with the group to finalize the private house sizes, types, budget, energy usage, and room-by-room requirements. Rather than focusing on factors such as "a 5'x7' bathroom," they should address specific conditions such as "one sink vs two sinks," handicap access, and every small detail. These are form generators that allow us to translate the group's desires into an architectural reality.

To create thorough private house design criteria for neurodiverse communities, some questions that architects ask future residents can include but are not limited to:

- What are the appropriate unit sizes? Will these units be occupied by single households, or will they be shared between various households? Will there be any caretakers living in these units?
- How many people will be cooking in the kitchen at one moment in time? Is each person responsible for their own groceries and cooking?
- How much privacy will each resident have and need in the private house if it is shared?
- Do families expect to grow over time?
- Do the private house programmatic zones correspond with sensory zones?
- How big are the front porches for each unit type? How do they provide transitions between exterior public and interior private spaces?

Once each house typology is completed, the architect will work out preliminary floor plans and meet with households to review plans and decide upon revisions. The goal is to create the highest-value homes that meet your goals and budget.

Before the future residents start designing their private houses, The Cohousing Company always starts the Private House Design Workshop with a review of the Common House Floor Plans. This review not only ensures that all the prioritized common amenity spaces are included, but it also allows each private house design to be more efficient and economical.

Designing the private houses together is what makes them work. Everyone worries that participatory design wastes time on the contrary, it is the main mechanism to save time. Done together over three days total, the workshops create houses that fit individual needs and are the right sizes. They will be reconsidered less, remodeled less, and cost less.

Adjoined houses that are efficiently sized and designed. When future residents come together to design their houses, the end product is always better than it is when an individual does it alone.

Quimper Village *"A" Unit: efficiently sized, warm, and comforting*

Wolf Creek Lodge: *Scandinavian decoration style—incorporating warmth, light, and air*

The design closure workshop brings it all together. Of course, it can be more organic, and it doesn't have to be this well-planned out, but when it's not planned out, it takes more time and more money.

Everyone feels proud of what they have accomplished together at the design closure workshop. It is recommended that if you're going to make a high-functioning ecovillage, you first make a high-functioning cohousing community. Cohousing compels the group to make thoughtful, thorough, and fair decisions.

5. Schematic Design Closure Workshop

With the group and developer approvals of the first phase of schematic design, buildings will be located on the site, and the site plan can be adjusted accordingly. The architect provides drawings for the building elevations that include proposed materials, front and rear porch locations, color schemes, and key design details. At the end of this phase, the architect meets with the group to present the building elevations and other drawings for approval. The goal of this phase is to bring closure to the schematic design process. After this step, the plans made will not be revisited unless an outside source determines that changes are necessary.

As the Schematic Design Workshop comes to a close, the design team should begin to consider the following:

- Preliminary material choices
- Preliminary landscape concepts
- Study models, if appropriate
- Code research and coordination with regulating agencies (building department, planning department)
- Most importantly, how any new information has affected the final design

For colder climates and where land is expensive, an interior courtyard in a one-building solution can still provide a sense of togetherness that can be found in a village setting.

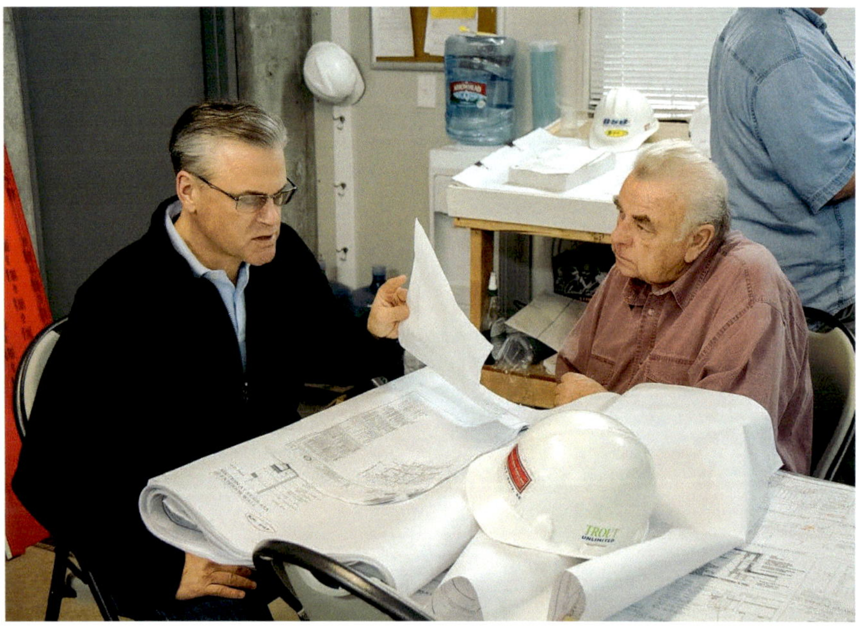

Overseeing construction is just as critical as anything else. You don't get what you expect, you get what you inspect.

Inevitably, there are unforeseen costs. Every amenity must be prioritized.

6. Design Development Workshop
Based on an approved Schematic Design, Design Development is the process of refining the design and working out all the details, including the selection of materials, colors, and engineering systems. The aim of the Design Development Workshop is to finalize material design decisions before proceeding with Construction Documents—the detailed and expensive documents that the contractor will need to complete the project.

A more detailed cost estimate may also be provided in this phase. In smaller projects, Design Development may become part of the Schematic and Construction Document phases rather than being a distinct phase of its own. The Design Development package will be reviewed with the client before proceeding with the project.

7. Prioritization Workshop
This is where costs are prioritized if the private and common amenities exceed the budget. Of course, there will be standard amenities provided in every home, but it is in the Prioritization Workshop where the architect determines what those are.

PERMITTING/FINANCING/ CONSTRUCTION

(The permitting, financing, and construction drawings efforts happen at the start of the Development and Design phases.)

1. Apply for Building Permits
When the working drawings are complete, the project is submitted to the building department for building permits. Allow several months for the building department to do plan checks.

2. Secure Construction Loan
The bank will review the financial pro forma, architectural drawings, number of committed buyers, required financial information, proof of site control, and planning approvals. Once the bank is convinced of the feasibility of the proposal, it will provide a "letter of intent" for the construction loan.

Keep in mind that there are two types of financing required to build a project.

1. A construction loan is a short-term loan required to pay for the actual construction of the project, as well as other development costs.
2. Permanent loans are the long-term mortgages held by the buyer(s), based on the individual financial statement(s). Members should be pre-qualified for permanent loans when the site is initially secured. Having pre-qualified buyers will also assist in securing the construction loan.

3. Negotiate Construction Contract
Once the construction documents (including specifications) are complete, the project is ready for contractors to bid on the costs to build the project. Your developer will often have a general contractor they prefer to work with; in some cases, the developer is also the general contractor. It is usually advantageous to work with a general contractor during the design phase to begin estimating costs.

4. Construction Financing in Place
Once the building department has approved the plans and the construction contract is finalized, your developer will finalize the construction loan with the bank.

The ground-breaking ceremony: this day marks the next phase of the community project.

"Going vertical," as the contractors like to call it.

Keeping your eyes on the prize means setting the builder up for success by not missing anything along the way.

Getting through the bureaucracies.

It's imperative to clarify the specific target population a project intends to serve. Is the project accommodating a mix of residents, people with certain disabilities, or another specific community?

It is also advantageous that these communities are developed with a wider cast of characters than just the residents and an architect, regardless of whether they're intended for neurotypical or neurodiverse people. Other contributors can be the parents and/or the funders; it is especially valuable to involve appropriate sociologists. However, it is critical to have the entire target population's full participation. You must ensure that *all* voices are being heard—not just the most outspoken ones. You can move blocks around; you can read body language. I have seen tears many times—they can be very telling.

Cohousing for Neurodivergent People

The path of least resistance for a family that wants to get their loved one into a community is to purchase a unit in a forming or newly built cohousing community. A four-bedroom house, for example, would work well: three bedrooms could go to adults with disabilities, and one could be designated for a caregiver. This was done in Bellingham Cohousing in Bellingham, WA. During the formation of this community, Kim's parents bought her a unit to live in with a couple of friends and a caregiver. Kim (20) is neurodivergent, but she functions successfully in the Bellingham Cohousing community, which is mostly neurotypical. Her parents visit to assist Kim with fulfilling community and work-share responsibilities—like cooking common meals and landscaping—but she is mostly able to function with the help of her housemates, caregiver, and the cohousing community without much assistance from her family.

Another option is to buy a unit in a pre-existing cohousing community. While it is not the cohousing residents' responsibility to care for the newcomer with disabilities, it is very likely that mutual support will develop over time. Thorough conversations and a community-wide agreement must happen before moving in.

Both arrangements are all about the individual within the community—how to get them into a supportive and loving community without taking advantage of anybody. In both cases, a real estate transaction must happen, but the community aspect is the driver. These two options will not give neurodiverse people the same level of community as they can get living in a village like Sólheimar, where most of their peers have intellectual disabilities like autism or Down syndrome. In that setting, it is easier to prioritize purpose through appropriate jobs, peer-to-peer cooperation, and peer-to-peer support. It's easier to get the right sociologists involved and easier to get people motivated; pride and purpose can be better accomplished. It's easier to achieve a sense of belonging, "I belong to that community." It's easier to achieve accountability, establish rules, and get them broadly accepted. It's easier to maintain a sense of identity. In a community built from the ground up, you can say, "Here, we have jobs, friends, and responsibilities." Most importantly, people are "at home" in their community during the day rather than away at work, school, etc. They are cared for, and they care for others.

This preliminary drawing embodies the hard work that the residents have put in throughout the various design workshops. It's an important milestone where they see their visions come to life.

Common Exit Strategy Scenarios for Mom and Dad

Scenario 1: Dad dies, and mom's caregiver must also now take care of "Junior." Mom dies (she owned the house), so the caregiver gets free rent to take care of Junior. Worst-case scenario: abuse, fraud, extortion, abandonment. Best-case scenario: neglect, isolation.

Scenario 2: Special needs trust (very expensive) takes up all of your free time and ultimately works poorly. Expensive lawyers are required, and there are many contingencies—"Who will Junior be passed on to?"—that never get resolved. "If you don't like it, then you take care of Junior," the caregiver says to Junior's older brother.

Scenario 3: Junior is homeless.

Scenario 4: Junior moves into a shared house that doesn't work.

Scenario 5: Junior moves in with a distant relative and that doesn't work.

Scenario 6: Junior gets sent off to a private company that gets bought out. The nursing staff is underpaid, undertrained, and unmotivated. The care facility closes, at least temporarily.

Scenario 7: Junior gets hospitalized, over-medicated, secluded, and misunderstood.

Scenario 8: Build a community. Community works because it presents a predictable scenario that provides love and true care.

A multi-stakeholder collaboration is when municipalities, professionals, educators, and others each play a role in defining the appropriate elements of a safe and supportive environment that meets the unique needs of the specific target group. Economical, optimal, and humanistic solutions can lead the way when there is public participation. The future of cohousing for disabled people must be one that is aimed at true therapeutic and community care. Advocating for this will require substantial grassroots and legislative efforts, but it's doable.

Include the future residents in the creation of design criteria, as every aspect of the design should be informed by this diverse population. Everyone has a little architect in them. They'll figure out what the common facilities should look like, all the way down to the dishes and the silverware. All the distinct common and private features will have a rhyme and a reason.

Real community is the secret ingredient to the feeling of belonging. Community is the secret ingredient to sustainability, affordability, feasibility, and every other-ility prefix I can think of: vulnerability, accountability, and more—need I go on? This book is almost out of words—it's time to stop reading and get on the Google machine. Tell everyone you know, "I care deeply about this, and if you do too, then you'll come to a public presentation 60 days from now about a potential new community in our town for folks who need and want some happiness." Better yet, get them to help you organize it. Around 200 people will come to hear a 1½ hour presentation and discussion on Thursday, then on Saturday morning, you will gather for a three-hour meeting about the next steps with 30–40 of the folks who are motivated to get started.

Scenario 8 is what this book is about. It's time to do it for yourself, for your son, for your daughter, and for the rest of the family. It's time to get this scenario adopted and implemented broadly in North America. Do it for all of the young adults who are ready to embrace life and for all of the parents who feel stuck. It's extremely disheartening to see young people with too little community.

Take this journey with others, and feel the emotional relief and the collective hope of getting somewhere *together*. The virtue of your success will be realized through the connections you discover with others and will be impactful for generations to come. This type of community is extremely doable, and no one else is going to do it for you, and it wouldn't be exactly how you envisioned it to be if they did. In fact, it likely wouldn't be built at all. We would accomplish less than "One Life, Live It!" Having built two high-functioning neighborhoods that I have lived in for the last 30 years, I can attest that the immense satisfaction and appreciation in these communities make the bumps in the road and the micro-dramas in the rear-view mirror seem trivial. These cohousing communities provide extreme gratification in living this one life we have; if not now, when?

APPENDICES

Appendix A

An Essential Further Reading: Somebody Somewhere: Breaking Free from The World of Autism by Donna Williams (1994)

As an architect launching into a book on this matter and designing environments for the neurodivergent population, many good folks—mostly folks with autistic children who I was designing communities for—offered dozens and dozens of books about autism to me. I am certain that without these texts, no architect could possibly understand the depths of the issues at hand. They are all good books, but one stood above all else: *Somebody Somewhere: Breaking Free from the World of Autism* by Donna Williams. Donna—who preferred to go by "Polly"—was an autistic Australian woman who wrote extensively about her experiences with autism in *Somebody Somewhere* (published when she was 31 years old) as a sequel to her bestseller *Nobody Nowhere*, which she wrote when she was 24 years old. Donna suffered the slings, arrows, and stigmas that come with having autism. As a talented writer, she had insights that I could not have possibly imagined, and they come rapidly to the reader. She wrote *Somebody Somewhere* at an age when the average person with autism thinks, "it might be time to get out of the house and go to 'the home;'" the age when their parents might come to an architect and ask, "what living arrangement can I get my son or daughter into that will be healthy for them after I am gone? Let's start planning it now" (the first step I suggest taking for these folks is to find other parents in the same position—see Chapter 10).

"All of my words come from TV," Donna says. "I had no other life to mimic." The teenage years are already hard to navigate. "Who am I?", "Where do I belong?", "Who might I become?" When there are no peers around, no clear and accepting company or community, then you very well might be lost until you find yourself—as Donna did. Through her writing, she began to understand what she and everyone she knew with autism in their 20s was missing: a community. Donna finally met other "kids" who also had autism, and together, they found a place to relax, accept one another, and learn from each other that had never previously existed for them.

In Donna's writing, there are no rules. It goes back and forth between imaginary and real characters; occasionally, a little fiction is required to tell the truth—the truth that had developed in her own heart. But with the help of others with autism, she found a clearer nonfictional truth and learned to navigate with it. Donna's book is not a stream of consciousness at all but simply portrays her authentic self: connecting, analyzing, and hurting.

"Without question or personal identification, I was in a state of total alienation. This, for me, was autism." She mimicked the sounds and motions of others without any thought whatsoever about what was heard or seen. "But I couldn't mimic life," the aggregate sum of coherency.

Donna characterizes seven other people who have autism—two of them fictional.

> *Carol and Willie were my 'more real' inner family, the characters I had created and through whom I had lived most of my past twenty-five years . . . Willie was a walking encyclopedia. Willie was amazingly strong and afraid of nothing. He was impervious to pain, physical or mental. When I channeled Willie, I could interact with and tolerate the world, while I stayed in my cage and did not. That was him talking, not me. When Willie was around, I was not scared to walk alone.*

> *Carol was my world family, the family that made me feel like I was part of the Brady Bunch. Carol came along a year and a half after Willie. Based on a little girl I met only once in the park; she had the role of being someone's darling child. Carol knows how to live in the world. I could never get into her world, but I could channel her behavior.*

"Self-abuse became my outward sign," Donna wrote, "Take me home, take me home, it's too hard out here," she desperately repeated to silence her mind.

From her perspective, achieving normality could never be accomplished, but she chased it nonetheless.

> *The appearance of normality meant survival. And you will never achieve normality unless you eat, breathe, sleep, and poop normality. And if you don't you will be treated as less than zero and possibly not be able to survive at all.*

> *Take away a full awareness of the world, the self is drained by overload. When it dares to come back, it is faced by the same challenges.*

Early on, she was diagnosed as "severely retarded with autistic tendencies." "It seemed that I was exceptional in some areas and very backward in others. I was born a genius and retarded." To her, normal people all looked alike, acted alike, and sounded alike. And being alike was a difficulty for her.

She felt like she was always at war with the world and had to remind herself over and over that there were no sides here—*it's not me against all of them.* But she always came back to the war as her default view of the world. Every time she walked into a room, she had to remind herself that there was no threat. Then she would become busy taking in every detail: the blinds, the chairs and their position, the tables, the art, the marks on the floor, the rugs, and so on—rapidly, if not instantaneously. She was always fighting the monster inside of herself; "when someone speaks to me, it's hard to grasp what they said because I was too busy noting and re-noting where the door was."

For too much of her young adult life, explaining herself was more difficult than just running all the time.

> *Anyway, what life is about is finding a place where you can be comfortable and*

safe and it doesn't mess you up or use parts of you while leaving the rest to die.

I finally got a job as a house cleaner—right in the middle of my capabilities, but a job I could hold.

From her first book, she learned that there are two ways to survive: to be nobody, nowhere, frozen and unable to do anything, or to do everything based on stored repertoire. Sleepwalking became a choice. She was swimming in a life of judgment and chaos. A small dig is a big dig; it was hard to listen. She could not stand high-pitched voices. In eight years, she had eight car accidents; only Donna ever got hurt. Survival meant living in a dream. But to appear to function was no longer an acceptable exchange for truly living: "I had to accept the harsh reality that to live would involve being so much less than I could be and more difficult than sleepwalking."

Donna harbored considerable contempt for "the world." It seemed that even when she communicated to "the world" that she was lactose intolerant (for example), the world would react as if "it's all in your head." Over and over, it seemed that if someone else from "the world" said that they were lactose intolerant or had any other allergies, they seemed to be accommodated. "It was impossible to build community;" there just weren't any opportunities. Community came in the way of blue uniforms.

Whenever I checked in, the hospital kept me for a minimum of two days—with the intent of no self-harm. There are other victims of this syndrome. Most of their mothers, who saw their child isolated and saw the pervasive societal ignorance. They lived with shame, guilt, and emotional exhaustion.

Donna illustrated that others with autism had the same anguishing frustration that plagued her own life. Jack's, Jody's, Michael's, Robert's, and so many others' lives were left on the table, so to speak. Their hearts and souls were left to watch TV, surf the net, stare at the ceiling, wonder and cry, perseverate, ruminate, and persevere. This review does not bring justice to the eloquence of Donna Williams' book—only you, the reader, can discover that for yourself. Look into the head and heart of a person with autism, and you will understand why I am writing this book, this call to action.

As a talented writer with autism, Donna Williams told a revealing story. Unfortunately, she passed away at the age of 53 from cancer. A true talent was lost. Thank you, Donna, for your amazing insights, humor, candor, and readability. Some books are fun to read despite the subject; yours is gripping. Thanks for sharing your genuine and powerful experiences of living with autism.

Appendix B

Attention Deficit Hyperactivity Disorder (ADHD)

This appendix is to better understand the author's motivation for this book and to discuss one of the other 200 possible diagnoses to be considered for the community. Of the additional 200 diagnoses, there are some that will work well together in the community, and there are some that will not. This notion is based on empirical data. It will be a fascinating book that discovers which diagnoses best commingle and which ones do not—unfortunately, that book does not yet exist. This author believes that at least one diagnosis resonates with every person. In one community designed by The Cohousing Company, the parents asked to accommodate folks with an IQ of 50–70 right next to another community for folks with an IQ of 70–90. They didn't want any caregivers or parents on site; they hoped it would be self-sufficient. There is a community for almost everyone, regardless of their diagnosis, we just have to figure it out.

One of the reasons I have a particular interest in the topics covered in this book is that I was diagnosed with severe ADHD by three separate psychologists and neurologists. Living with ADHD is a challenge; I look and (usually) act normal, but sometimes I grow too impatient to carry on a "normal" conversation. Most people—including myself until recently—won't discuss their own mental health. They fear the stigma and judgment, but I feel it needed to be mentioned here.

ADHD is not debilitating for all of those affected, but it gives you a bizarre perspective on life. At the very least, it changes your life trajectory. You do things impulsively, and sometimes you say things impulsively.

In the U.S., approximately two-thirds of young offenders and one-half of the adult prison population have ADHD or ADHD symptoms. They do things inappropriately, like taking things simply because they want them or hitting people when they are angry. However, many successful business and social entrepreneurs also have ADHD. They don't have the time to wait; if they see an opportunity in the marketplace or to build a better society, they jump on it. I saw that we needed appropriate furniture for children in the childcare centers that our office was designing, so I started designing it immediately and got it to a factory to begin production. I saw the need for childcare centers in San Francisco, and with the help of Mayor Dianne Feinstein and the City of San Francisco, we built 17 new childcare centers over the span of two and a half years. I have witnessed many completely dysfunctional neighborhoods in California—in North America in general—and have championed a campaign to bring high-functioning neighborhoods back. I coined the word cohousing, initiated the cohousing movement in the U.S., designed 55 model high-functioning neighborhoods, and wrote 15 books on the topic. I received the Prize for Social Innovation as Social Innovator of the Year in 1992 by the Institute for Social Innovations in London and have won the Human Habitat Award presented by the United Nations. And now, I'm motivated to see high-functioning communities get built for neurologically diverse and divergent populations.

ADHD is a condition accompanied by many challenges in life, but it can also be a valuable asset. When it comes to creating a healthier society, sometimes it pays to be impatient—and impatience is one of the main symptoms of ADHD, accompanied by hyperactivity, inattention, and impulsivity.

In my mind, telling people that you have ADHD is like telling people that you have narcolepsy—I might fall asleep in the middle of our conversation; please don't take it personally. I mostly get impatient with people who don't see the need to do things differently. But I'm excited and inspired by those who want to make progress.

They say that if you have ADHD, it's likely that you're very good at one thing. You can focus (under the right circumstances and motivations), drill down, understand one concept in great detail, and see things that others can't. Michael Phelps, a 28-time Olympic medalist, is a perfect example; he visualizes his swim like a savant. Karina Smirnoff is a five-time national dancing champion and world champion; she channels focus to acute nuances in her movement, and she visualizes every body part in motion. Simone Biles—gravity-defying gymnast and eleven-time Olympic medalist—was once disqualified for her ADHD medications. Solange Knowles is an amazing singer, songwriter, and artist; she knows a lot of people who start things that they don't finish, people who go places and get lost, people who have trouble following verbal or written directions—people who have

ADHD just like she does. We are the ones who have trouble paying attention and staying organized and, most reputably, can't sit still. Solange compensates when singing because of her acute ability to focus during a single moment on one thing. It is widely believed that J.K. Rowling has ADHD. Her practice of filling up cardboard boxes with 3x5 cards (her draft manuscript) and then pulling them out one by one to craft the story is a pretty good indication.

Architecture is the one thing that I focus on; I articulate every detail necessary to get successful buildings and communities built. I "see" where every drop of water travels, and I see every nuance to the aggregate sum of the people in the room and their involvement in the culture. ADHD is a weird neurodevelopmental disorder affecting the brain and nervous system. All of this exemplifies the fact that it takes a village to complement all the skills and symptoms that folks with ADHD have. I can hyperfocus on architecture, color, details, sound waves, and people because these are what I'm interested in. But I need my community to help me see the bigger picture.

ADHD Symptoms that Affect Relationships with Neighbors, Family, and Associates Include

Being inattentive, easily distracted, hyperactive; getting bored quickly; being impulsive and impatient; not listening when being spoken to; daydreaming; difficulty following instructions; often shaking somewhere (usually a leg); talking too much; interrupting other people; using inappropriate levels and tone of voice; getting lost easily and having trouble with cognitive mapping; eating compulsively. People with ADHD often experience fluctuations in mood, behavior, and mindset. They are normally hunters, not gatherers. The plate in front of them is easy prey; eating is easy stimulation. The condition is so pervasive and the symptoms so varied and sometimes disruptive that hundreds of books are written on the topic.

Best Practices for Neighbors, Teachers, and Families for Dealing with Someone with ADHD

> *1. Empathy is always the best tactic.*
>
> *2. Objective goals: do not raise your voice, and work persistently on maintaining patience.*

Luckily, today, I live in a cohousing community where my neighbors are direct and honest. This has pushed me to work hard on being more introspective and conscious of what I do and say. While cohousers are often thoughtful, deliberate, and careful, they can have a hard time with someone who is impulsive and interrupts others—there is always some compromise. People with ADHD sometimes do things too rapidly. In my experience, one or two folks with ADHD in a cohousing community can work, but only if individuals in the community are empathetic and if those with ADHD are willing to be intentional and work hard at keeping their compulsive behavior in check.

All of the various diagnoses must have their specific communities re-optimized in order to be successful. Some may have ADHD, while others are diagnosed differently; there's an algorithm in our future.

No one is left out here; there are about 200 diagnoses to consider. It will be a lot of work to figure out how to best accommodate each, but this study will be a book for another day. It is not yet known which diagnosis will thrive naturally in the community and which ones will have to be more carefully considered. Cerebral Palsy, Schizophrenia, depression, anxiety disorders, post-traumatic stress disorders—some communities embracing these disorders will thrive, and some will only thrive with a considerably conscious and honest approach. It is better to be completely objective and deliberate about these matters, as the future lives of affected people are at stake.

By virtue of Sólheimar and comparable communities, the world is recognizing that what is humane is community; what is sustainable is community; what is economical is community. What is not smart or justifiable is isolating people in their bedrooms. Our default approaches of "home alone," institutionalization, or even shared housing need to be carefully reconsidered. The time is now to figure out what other diagnoses could thrive in cohousing.

I have noticed in several cohousing projects that folks with Seasonal Affective Disorder (SAD), as well as PTSD and other stress/trauma-related disorders, can thrive very well in neurotypical cohousing. However, a high-functioning cohousing community is required to make a positive difference for everyone.

There was a young man living in a cohousing community in Denmark that I lived in for six months. He was so hyperactive, aberrant, and challenging that I thought for sure he was eventually headed for prison. Luckily, he lived in cohousing where everyone understood his condition; they were extraordinarily patient with him. He grew up, moved out, mellowed a bit, went to college, mellowed more, became a successful tech entrepreneur, and has now moved back to the same community with his young family. He demonstrated what I have witnessed thousands of times: challenged folks need patient, empathetic people around them to succeed. Acceptance and empathy seem to be the necessary ingredients for encouraging people to find their own success eventually. That young man was one of the motivations to write my first book about cohousing communities—a place for aberrant children to be known and loved by neighbors and peers. In general, challenged populations such as those with autism, Down syndrome, and ADHD need patient, empathetic people willing to communicate with them and attempt to understand them.

Appendix C

Statistics Compiled by Autism Parenting Magazine 2024

by Irene Masteller

General Facts

- An estimated 2.2% of adults (5.7 million) and 2.8% of children (2.1 million) in the U.S. are autistic
- Autism occurs in all socioeconomic groups

Causes and Risk Factors

- A child has an approximately 19% higher risk of autism if an older sibling is on the spectrum; autism has a strong genetic component, as demonstrated by twin studies
- Maternal infection, drug use, and parental age may be contributing factors to the development of autism
- Health complications during pregnancy and childbirth may increase a child's autism risk by 44%
- Although toxins in the environment, especially heavy metals like mercury and lead, have been associated with an increased risk, most of these studies have various methodological limitations, and it is yet to be conclusively determined

Conditions and Risks Associated with Autism

- Research suggests around 40% of autistic children and adolescents have at least one comorbid *anxiety* disorder
- Roughly half of all children with ASD may also experience symptoms of ADHD
- Up to 90% of autistic individuals may have atypical sensory experiences
- Children on the spectrum are more likely than neurotypical peers to experience sleep, gastrointestinal, and weight management challenges
- Autistic children are 160x more likely to die from drowning in comparison to the general pediatric population; individuals on the spectrum have a substantially heightened risk of dying from serious injury
- Children on the spectrum are more likely than neurotypical peers to be the victim of bullying; autistic children are twice as likely (as children who don't have the condition) to report suicidal thoughts. Research suggests that deficits in social communication may lead to a lack of emotional connectivity, which elevates the risk of suicide

Children

- Almost 3 million children under the age of 18 have autism in the U.S. (one in every 36 kids)
- Boys are nearly four times more likely to be diagnosed than girls
- A recent study found that compared with non-Hispanic White children, autism prevalence was 1.8 times as high among Hispanic children and 1.6 times as high among non-Hispanic Black children
- Although autism can be diagnosed before a child reaches the age of two, most kids are diagnosed only after the age of 4
- Many children with autism are nonverbal (around 40%) and struggle to communicate effectively
- 44% have average or above-average intellectual ability
- 31% have an intellectual disability
- Rates of autism vary from state to state; the state with the highest rates of autism measured in the U.S. is California (3.9%) and the lowest in Missouri (1.7%)
- Autism prevalence rates in children vary across the globe: 2.6% in South Korea, 0.36% in France, and 1.17% in Qatar. Many countries do not have reliable autism statistics due to a lack of resources. The World Health Organization (WHO) estimates that, on average, 1 in every 100 children has autism globally, but this estimate is likely low due to many factors.
- Why is there so much variation between countries and even between states? Do areas with higher prevalence rates have parents who are better educated and more aware of autism? Alternatively, are these areas with higher prevalence rates more accepting of neurodivergence, creating an environment where seeking diagnosis and intervention is easier with less stigma? We need more research, but autism prevalence per country does seem to be influenced by the following:
  - ◊ *Autism education, awareness and acceptance*
  - ◊ *Better diagnostic practices*
  - ◊ *Changes in diagnostic criteria*

Parents and Caregiving Stress

- Almost a fifth of parents with a child on the autism spectrum have symptoms of PTSD.
- The overall prevalence of anxiety and depressive symptoms is elevated in mothers of autistic children. A study found depressive symptoms in 72.5% and anxiety in 80.2% of participating mothers—67.1% suffered from both symptoms.
- A study looking at support needs of parents with autistic children found mothers and fathers emphasized different aspects of support.
- It's important to remember parents with kids on the spectrum also require extensive support.
- Parents with autistic children experience more stress than

parents with neurotypical children and parents with children with other developmental disorders. Stress levels are influenced by several factors, including parent characteristics, child characteristics, family and social support systems, professional support, socioeconomic status.

- Extra costs for autistic children are mainly driven by special education needs (37.2%) and loss in parental productivity (28.4%).
- Considering the high cost of raising a child in our current system, 25%–45% of parents declare reducing working hours or stopping work altogether.
- Parents worry about their autistic child's future and their own ability to care for their child as they age.
- A study suggests that although parents are aware of the need to plan for their child's future, many have trouble initiating such planning.
- The study further suggests social workers need to be educated to help parents plan and separate planning into manageable bits while supporting parents through each stage of the planning. *This is a big asset of Sólheimar. Social workers who live there help residents every day.*

"Hope, Growth, and Possibilities" Treatment/Intervention/Support

- A study found that most of the participating children with severe language delays go on to acquire language skills with language therapy
  - ◊ 43% became fluent speakers
  - ◊ 70% could speak in simple phrases
- More than 3/4 of school-age autistic children are doing well in at least one of the five developmental areas by the age of 10, and nearly 1/4 are doing well in all five developmental areas
- While FDA-approved medication for treating irritability in autism is limited to risperidone and aripiprazole, caregivers are increasingly turning to complementary and alternative medications (such as CBD to treat anxiety and challenging behavior)
- Kids need support from family, educators, medical professionals, therapists, and *the community* to thrive
- A 2023 meta-analysis by the National Institute of Health states that 20% of autistic children and teens reported suicidal ideation in the past year, and 10% reported suicide attempts. Non-autistic children and teens comparatively report rates of 14.2% for suicidal thoughts and 4.5% for suicidal attempts

Afterword

After the first edition of the book, *The Senior Cohousing Handbook: A Community Approach to Independent Living,* was published in 2005, I asked the readers to please let me know which topics they felt were not adequately covered. Specifically, what topics in their view were not addressed and are needed to better determine how to make a senior community for themselves in their town?

The first edition of The Senior Cohousing Handbook inspired half a dozen early adopters to get their senior cohousing project built, which was great. However, with the feedback from the first book implemented into the second edition released in 2009, a movement began—dozens of state-of-the-art senior cohousing communities have now been built in North America. Even these books are participatory!

Years later, I went to Iceland to study the best cultural environment that I knew of for intellectually and neurologically diverse people, a positive political environment largely inspired by Sólheimar.

For the second edition of this book, I am asking the larger neurodiverse community to offer specific questions and feedback about the Sólheimar Community: what are the best practices we can use to bring this type of high-functioning community to our country/place? If there is information you believe to be superfluous, distracting, inaccurate, or unnecessary, please note it. Feedback is especially helpful in the following forms:

1. Any wisdom you might have that would help a mom and or dad imagine that a community setting might be best for the short-term and long-term well-being of their son or daughter.
2. There are redundancies in this book. When I felt strongly about making a point, I guess I had to say it twice. But I understand this repetition can be distracting, so please let me know where saying it twice (or 12 times) really doesn't work.
3. Any verbiage that is just too squishy (isn't it wonderful) and does not really contribute to the core message.
4. The language is just too strong—controversial or even righteous. I don't want to turn people off with too strident language.
5. When you believe that a different turn-of-phrase would be more communicative: "A community is a place where everyone knows each other, cares about each other, and supports each other." If you can think of a better or more articulate way to say that, I'd love to hear it.

This book is responding to many concerned parents who asked: "How do we get something like the Sólheimar community built for our son?"; "Our 30-year-old son can get along, or at least get by; or should I say survive? But we want him to thrive and be happy."; "How can I make something like this possible in the region where I live?"

When we know that an autistic child could function in a community of peers and friends if it were properly organized, even if we are not physically in it, we can and need to do it now!

If we are to evolve to become a better society, the future must include providing supportive environments for folks to take better care of themselves and each other. We must create these environments ourselves. Projects like the Sólheimar community start with one person with vision, hope, and determination to make it happen.

Anyone interested in the concept of better housing for intellectually challenged and neurodiverse folks is invited to help with the second edition of this book by forwarding their questions and suggestions; please e-mail me at charles.durrett@cohousingco.com

Chuck Durrett

Glossary

Anthroposophy
A spiritual movement inspired by the teachings and writings of German philosopher, architect, and theosophist Rudolf Steiner. Etymologically, it derives from the Greek words for human (Anthropos) and wisdom (Sophia), asserting that there is a fundamental wisdom that all humans possess. Today, it has inspired alternative, holistic pedagogical approaches, such as the Waldorf schools of Europe and North America as well as those listed in this book. It has also drawn a good deal of criticism due to the racist ideologies of its founder, Steiner.

Cohousing
Cohousing is basically custom high-functioning neighborhoods designed to be great places for children to grow up and for seniors to grow old. Great places to be a parent and great places to be a teenager—if there is such timing. One teenager in Nevada City Cohousing wrote in a senior essay, "If you grew up in a cohousing, I don't think you'll ever use drugs—there are no holes in your heart."

Comorbidity
The presence of two or more disabilities or diseases within a person.

Infill
Developing the underutilized or undeveloped space on a lot that already contains built elements.

Intellectual/Developmental Disabilities and Disorders (I/DD)
Conditions at birth that uniquely affect the trajectory of the individual's physical, intellectual, and/or emotional development. Many of these conditions affect multiple body parts or systems. Mentioned in this book are:

1. **Autism spectrum disorder (ASD):** A developmental disability that can cause significant social, communication, and behavioral challenges. People with ASD might repeat certain behaviors and might not want change in their daily activities.
2. **Asperger syndrome:** A developmental disorder formerly characterized by difficulties in social interaction and nonverbal communication, along with restricted and repetitive patterns of behavior and interests. It is no longer recognized as a separate, distinct diagnosis and has been folded into the ASD classification.
3. **Cerebral palsy (CP):** A group of disorders that affect a person's ability to move and maintain balance and posture. It is the most common disability in childhood.
4. **Down syndrome:** The result of an extra chromosome. There are trillions of cells in the human body. They are so tiny you can only see them through a microscope. Inside these tiny cells are even tinier parts called chromosomes. Most people have 46 chromosomes in each of their cells. People with Down syndrome have 47, and because of that, they may look and learn differently.
5. **Dementia:** The development of multiple cognitive deficits that include memory impairment and potentially aphasia, apraxia, agnosia, or a disturbance in executive functioning. It is not a specific disease but rather a descriptor for a group of symptoms. Alzheimer's is the most common form of dementia. A degenerative brain disorder that worsens with time. The most common early symptom is difficulty remembering newly learned information, eventually leading to difficulties remembering time and place, family and friends, events, etc. It may also lead to loss of motor functions.
6. **Obsessive-Compulsive Disorder (OCD):** A long-lasting disorder in which a person experiences uncontrollable and recurring thoughts (obsessions), engages in repetitive behaviors (compulsions), or both. Symptoms are time-consuming and can cause significant distress or interfere with daily life.

Ecovillage
An intentional community planned through a participatory process that integrates social well-being and economic and environmental sustainability as a core component of its operation.

Gentle Teaching
A pedagogical philosophy that affirms the belief that every individual, regardless of their abilities or challenges, has the capacity for positive change and connection with one another. Gentle Teaching incorporates compassion as an alternative to the reactive and restrictive practices that are commonplace in working with those who have complex needs. Using positive reinforcement, touch, understanding, and love, Gentle Teaching creates a safe environment in which all people can be comfortable with themselves.

Gift Economy
Material and commodified wealth are replaced by the real wealth that community brings. In a normal market, you create something and sell it for more than the effort that was expended to make it so you can spend that excess of other people's surplus. In the gift economy, you rely on others to help you with what you need, and they rely on you at no extra expense.

Home People
This is what the residents of Sólheimar refer to themselves as.

Horizontal Management
The deliberate, direct involvement of the members of an organization, community, or institution in its planning and operation.

Hygge (pron. hooga)
A Danish concept that describes a warm, comfortable environment; the atmosphere that gives respite from the craziness of the day.

Programming
The criteria and conditions that inform how a community will be/is designed. These include climatic factors, social factors, site-specific physical restraints, etc. This is the most important step in the design process. Good programming allows the community to fit like a glove for its inhabitants.

Reverse Integration
Creating an environment where the neurotypical population adjusts to neurodiverse communities rather than the other way around.

Support Intensity Scale
A standardized assessment tool that assists in determining how much assistance a person with a developmental disability needs in community settings.

Level 1 "Requiring support"

Social communication:
Without supports in place, deficits in social communication cause noticeable impairments. Difficulty initiating social interactions and clear examples of atypical or unsuccessful responses to social overtures of others. May appear to have decreased interest in social interactions. For example, a person who is able to speak in full sentences and engages in communication but whose to-and-fro conversation with others fails and whose attempts to make friends are odd and typically unsuccessful.

Restricted, repetitive behaviors:
Inflexibility of behavior causes significant interference with functioning in one or more contexts. Difficulty switching between activities. Problems of organization and planning hamper independence.

Some diagnoses respond better to the value of community and relationships better than others. That said, it truly is a person-by-person question. That is, you never know until you introduce a person and let them try it for a while. Some reject it immediately.

In the case of Sólheimar, it is not just the connections that matter and "bringing people out of their shell," which happens more often than we can imagine, but also people are helped along with the value of community.

Level 2 "Requiring substantial support"

Social communication:
Marked deficits in verbal and nonverbal social communication skills: social impairments apparent even with supports in place, limited initiation of social interactions, and reduced or abnormal responses to social overtures from others. For example, a person who speaks simple sentences, whose interaction is limited to narrow special interests, and who has markedly odd nonverbal communication.

Restricted, repetitive behaviors:
Inflexibility of behavior, difficulty coping with change, or other restricted/ repetitive behaviors appear frequently enough to be obvious to the casual

observer and interfere with functioning in a variety of contexts. Distress and// or difficulty changing focus or action.

Level 3 "Requiring very substantial support"

Social communication:
Severe deficits in verbal and nonverbal social communication skills cause severe impairments in functioning, very limited initiation of social interactions, and minimal response to social overtures from others. For example, a person with few words of intelligible speech who rarely initiates interaction and, when he or she does, makes unusual approaches to meet needs only and responds to only very direct social approaches.

Restricted, repetitive behaviors:
Inflexibility of behavior, extreme difficulty coping with change, or other restricted/repetitive behaviors markedly interfere with functioning in all spheres. Great distress/difficulty changing focus or action.

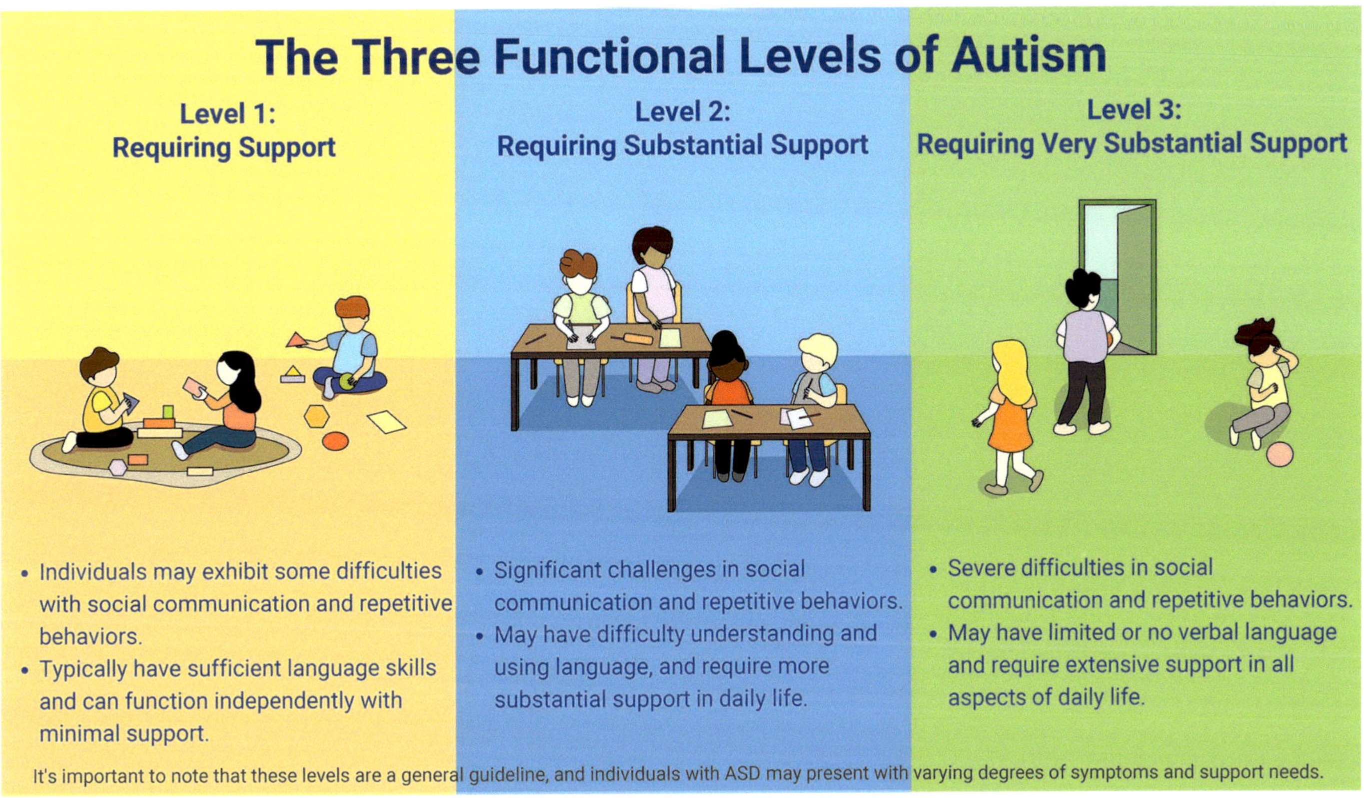

Index

For Product Safety Concerns and Information,
please contact our EU representative GPSR@taylorandfrancis.com
Taylor & Francis Verlag GmbH, Kaufingerstraße 24,
80331 München, Germany

Printed by Integrated Books International,
United States of America